THE 4400

™

THE OFFICIAL COMPANION
SEASONS 1 AND 2

The 4400: The Official Companion
Seasons 1 and 2

ISBN-10: 1 84576 473 0
ISBN-13: 9781845764739

Published by
Titan Books
A division of
Titan Publishing Group Ltd
144 Southwark St
London
SE1 0UP

First edition July 2007
10 9 8 7 6 5 4 3 2 1

DEDICATION
To the woman who gives me reason to write, smile and sigh, my beloved wife and partner in all things literary, Paula M. Block.

ACKNOWLEDGEMENTS
One day I innocently answered the phone to hear a voice say, "Boy, are you in trouble now." "What?" I asked, unsure whether to be humored or horrified. The voice replied, "Ira Behr asked for you to author *The 4400 Companion.*" That call led to dozens of others, which in turn led to transcribing and writing and photo gathering of all the material you're holding in your hands. And yet, so far at least, it's been no trouble at all. While a simple mass 'thank you' seems inadequate, it's all I've got, so here goes —
    Thank you to Ira Steven Behr, Maira Suro, Scott Peters, and the rest of the writers, producers and filmmakers on *The 4400*. And thank you to Joel Gretsch, Jacqui McKenzie, and their fellow cast members for kindly lending their thoughts, insights and time to this project. Your words are inside — aren't you glad you took my call?!
    Thank you also to Jeff Wachtel and Jackie de Crinis at USA Network: we've doubled the fun. A special thanks for going one step beyond to Magdelana Campbell, Adam Levy, Jeff Pickett, Christin Scholten and Neil Williams. Thank you to the very helpful group at CBS Consumer Products. And thank you to Jo Boylett for being my outstanding, understanding and still standing editor at Titan Books.

Titan Books would also like to thank the cast and crew of *The 4400*, in particular Ira Steven Behr and Scott Peters for the Foreword and Afterword. We're also grateful to Paula Block and John Van Citters at CBS for their continuing help and support of this project.

Visit our website:
www.titanbooks.com

Did you enjoy this book? We love to hear from our readers. Please e-mail us at:
readerfeedback@titanemail.com or write to Reader Feedback at the above address.

To subscribe to our regular newsletter for up-to-the-minute news, great offers and competitions, email:
booksezine@titanemail.com

A CIP catalogue record for this title is available from the British Library.

Printed and bound in Canada.

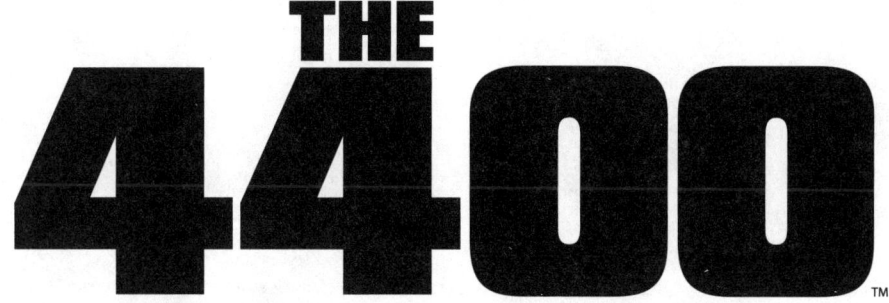

THE 4400

THE OFFICIAL COMPANION
SEASONS 1 AND 2

Terry J. Erdmann

The 4400 created by Scott Peters and René Echevarria

TITAN BOOKS

Contents

Foreword by Ira Steven Behr   6

A LIGHT IN THE SKY   8

MAIN CAST CREDITS   19

SEASON ONE   20

FROM MINISERIES TO SEASON TWO   42

SEASON TWO   46

CHARACTERS
    Tom Baldwin   98
    Diana Skouris   102
    Richard Tyler   106
    Lily Moore Tyler   110
    Shawn Farrell   114
    Kyle Baldwin   118
    Maia Rutledge Skouris   122
    Recurring Characters   126

BEHIND THE SCENES
    Production Design   138
    Music   145
    Visual Effects   151

Afterword by Scott Peters   158

People often ask me, "What's it like working on *The 4400*?" Next to, "Have you ever met William Shatner/Leonard Nimoy/DeForest Kelly/James Doohan/Walter Koenig/Nichelle Nichols?" it's probably the question I hear the most. (For those wondering, the answers would be: Yes/Yes/Yes/No/Yes/Not Sure.)

So, what's it like working on *The 4400*?

Well, for one thing, it's hard.

Not brain surgery hard.

Not ditch digging hard.

Not running into some dark alley after some crackhead with a glock hard.

But hard, nonetheless.

Which doesn't really tell you much, does it?

After all, your job isn't all lollipops and moonbeams either.

So, what's it like working on *The 4400*?

I guess it's a good thing you bought this book. Because that's what Terry Erdmann (and Paula Block) did. They tracked down everyone involved with the show who was willing to talk, and they asked them that question and dozens, sometimes hundreds, of others. So in the following pages you'll be discovering many different answers, many different points of view, not only from myself, but also from Joel, and Jackie, Patrick, Ali, Craig, Scott, Maira...

Okay — time out!

Here's where I start talking about how great the show is, how wonderful all my colleagues are, how insightful this book is... Where have you read that before? Try everywhere. Because that's what introductions to these sorts of books are all about. Self-congratulatory pats on the back to all involved, and earnest reassurances that you, dear reader, have spent your money wisely. Even if all that happens to be true, and I'm not saying otherwise, do you really need me to tell you that?

Frankly, I'd like to do better. I'd like you to do better. I'd like us to do better. So how about I share with you a truth that you won't find anywhere else in this book. What do you say we give that a try? Oh, and by the way, I do think I met Nichelle Nichols.

So, what's it like working on *The 4400*?

You know those rows and rows of sleepers in *The Matrix*. The first film? The good one?

It's like that.

Because working on *The 4400*, or any television series, is like a collective dream. The writers, the actors, the directors, editors, crew people, even the studio and network executives may all be working together — but more importantly they're all dreaming together. They take a vagary — an idea, a story, a script — they see words on a page, in their mind's eye, and they imagine it into reality. By believing in the make-believe they dream the show into existence. And then, as if by magic, and after twenty years I still wouldn't know how to walk you step-by-step through the process, the episodes are beamed from a studio, off a satellite, into your living room, through your TV set (hopefully a plasma/lcd/dlp/whatever type of big screen — invest in one, it's worth it) and directly into your brain. Which is where our dream becomes your dream.

And what better chimera, what more appropriate phantasm than 4400 people, returning in a ball of light, only to find themselves possessed of abilities profound and disquieting. And then learning they had been sent back from the future to save mankind.

So then, I think it's safe to say that what you're holding in your hand is that rarest of things, a book of dreams.

With maybe a nightmare or two thrown in for good measure.

And that's what it's like working on *The 4400*.

Come, dream along with me.

Ira Steven Behr
Executive Producer
December 2006

"We're not a threat; we're salvation. The world will have to deal with us." — **Jordan Collier**

In 2002, after a decade of writing and directing for television, Scott Peters found himself between jobs — and just a bit bored. "I'd hit a bit of a dry spell, and I was looking for a staff writing job," recalls the veteran of such series as *Are You Afraid of the Dark*, *Highlander* and *The Outer Limits*. "I wasn't interested in cop shows, but I kept getting called into meetings for them," he says with a sigh. "Eventually I decided to sit down and create a show of my own. The very first thing I typed into my computer was 'A Light In the Sky'. And then I wrote a few paragraphs to get the major premise down."

Peters' premise was bare-boned: an object appears in the sky over Earth and returns thousands of previously abducted "children". With "thousands" of returnees, Peters knew there'd be enough material to sustain a series.

What Peters *didn't* know was what the overall story would be, so, he admits, "I left those paragraphs in the computer for a while. I wanted to make sure it wouldn't end up only being about lead characters solving cases, like Mulder and Scully on *The X-Files*. I wanted it to be about who those lead characters were, who their families were, and what was going on in their lives. Things that I could savor for the entire run."

Of course, thinking that his concept might have a "run" at all may have been a bit presumptuous at the time. "I conceived it as serialized science fiction with an ensemble cast," Peters says, well aware that, at the time, such projects weren't appealing to budget-minded development executives. In fact, when Peters showed it to his reps, "They said, 'This is *fantastic*! It'll *never* sell!'"

Nevertheless, his manager called Maira Suro, then president of American Zoetrope Television, a division of Francis Ford Coppola's production company, who agreed to meet with Peters. Suro still recalls the opening of his pitch. "There's all this excitement over the comet," she relates, "and suddenly that turns into fear, with people getting on phones to say their goodbyes, and then the comet *stops* and there's a big explosion that leaves 4400 people who've been missing for up to sixty years. After he talked for about fifteen minutes, I said, 'Wow. That's a cool idea.'"

Opposite: Tom Baldwin (Joel Gretsch) and Diana Skouris (Jacqueline McKenzie) face their first encounter with forces from the future.

With Suro's guidance, the bare-boned premise quickly expanded. "Scott brought in all this great character stuff," Suro says, "including a kid in a coma, and his missing cousin." Soon they'd added elements such as the show's investigative aspect, the Homeland Security office, and the partnership between the main characters. After several months, Suro recalls, "All of the main characters weren't there yet, but we felt it was time to take it out."

Above: Kyle Baldwin (Chad Faust) and Shawn Farrell (Patrick Flueger), just before their lives take a dramatic turn.

Suro arranged for meetings at several production studios, including Fox Television. "The Fox meeting was my very first network pitch," says Peters. "And before we left their office, the Fox executives said, 'Yes. We want to do this.'"

But from that high point, the pair descended into the less thrilling process known in Hollywood as "development hell". From August 2002 until January 2003, "Scott and I worked very closely on numerous drafts of a one-hour script," says Suro. "But when Fox began the process of scheduling pilots for the coming season, they told us they didn't feel we were ready."

The studio executives suggested bringing in an additional writer, and introduced the pair to René Echevarria, whose credits included *Star Trek: The Next Generation*, *Star Trek: Deep Space Nine* and *Dark Angel*. "I was intrigued by the show's premise, and I loved the beginning," Echevarria remembers. But he recognized the need for changes and additions. "It started *hot*," he says, "with this thing coming and everyone saying goodbye. But then there was a time jump and a year had passed. There was a returnee, a senator's son with the ability to camouflage himself like a chameleon, who was murdering people. I set that aside and came up with Orson Bailey and his telekinetic ability."

Echevarria was bothered that every returnee in the script was living a "terrible" life. "I wondered if any of them might feel that the world they'd come back to might actually be a *better* place than the one they'd left," he relates. Noting that the senator's son had been a soldier in the Korean War, he incorporated that detail into a new character he called Richard. He then linked Richard to a young woman in the script named Lily, and revealed a mysterious connection between them: Lily's grandmother had been Richard's youthful sweetheart.

"René really loved the intimate storylines," Suro says. "He came up with that timeless romance between Lily and Richard, this lovely notion of two souls connected through her grandmother, who looked exactly like her.

"And then," Suro adds, "René came up with Maia. She was all his."

Several weeks later, "we pitched those changes to the executives at Fox, and they commissioned another draft of the script," reports Echevarria. But the trio had a problem. The studio was expecting a one-hour pilot, which translates into a script of approximately sixty pages. "But with all the stuff we'd included, it came to about seventy-five pages. We had to get it down to sixty — so Scott and I spent hours cheating the margins!"

Then came the bad news. The top executives at Fox, Suro states, "chose not to move forward with it." Fortunately, however, when the development deal had been negotiated, Zoetrope and its partner, Viacom Productions, had written in a clause claiming their right to retain ownership of the project. Not long after, American Zoetrope disbanded its television division, freeing Suro to become a full-time producer and concentrate on her favorite project. "I started sending the script out to the places where I felt it really had a shot. That's when I ended up calling Jeff Wachtel at USA."

The timing couldn't have been better for Wachtel, executive vice president of Original Programming at USA Network. "We needed a summer series," Wachtel says. "I read the script Maira sent me, and then passed it around. We all thought it was fantastic, so we set up a meeting with Maira, Scott and René. The penny dropped for

Above: Lily Moore (Laura Allen) and Richard Tyler (Mahershalalhashbaz Ali) kindle a timeless, and colorblind, romance.

Above: Little girl lost Maia Rutledge (Conchita Campbell) inexplicably knows that no one is coming to take her home.

me the moment René told us the end, that the returnees hadn't been abducted by aliens, but by humans from the future. It was a *great* concept."

But the selling point that ultimately guaranteed the project a home at USA was that "great character stuff" that had made such an impression on Suro when she first heard the premise. "We all fell in love with that aspect of the show we referred to internally at USA as 'life interrupted'," states Jackie de Crinis, senior vice president of Original Scripted Series at USA Network. "What if your life had been interrupted? If forty years have passed for everyone else, how do you reclaim your marriage, your job, your identity? We were so compelled by that personal drama that we didn't think very hard about the science fiction element. In fact, the science fiction was icing on the cake of what really was a good character drama."

Perry Simon, then President of Viacom Productions, agrees with de Crinis. "*The 4400* had all the great ingredients." And although the economics of basic cable networks can make production of science fiction a dicey proposition, Simon sought a way to make it work. "We came up with a double proposal," he explains. "We would do it as a limited series, so no one would be required to go forward unless it was successful enough that everyone felt comfortable. *And* we brought in Sky Television as a production partner. That enabled us to do a rather large budget basic cable show."

Wachtel recalls that he was able to give "a relatively quick green light" to a two-hour 'Pilot', leaving the writers with only weeks to turn their "one-hour" script (which actually timed out closer to ninety minutes) into a two-hour format. But the "limited series" that Simon had negotiated had a caveat. USA wasn't sure whether they would air the two-hour 'Pilot' as a one-off, or whether they would extend the project into a miniseries. To cover all bases, the network ordered four additional scripts, to be completed before the end of principal photography on the 'Pilot'. "If we loved the daily footage *and* the four scripts," Wachtel explains, "we would tell them to keep shooting."

Peters, Suro and Echevarria found themselves facing a cluster of dilemmas and deadlines. The two-hour 'Pilot' needed to have an ending that would be satisfying if it were ultimately broadcast as a stand-alone movie. But it also had to be open-ended, in case the network decided to turn it into the first chunk of a six-hour miniseries. Similarly, the four follow-up scripts had to culminate in an ending that would work if the show stopped at that point, but also had to stay open-ended enough to tantalize the viewers, should the ratings inspire a second season. One thing was obvious: they'd need to hire additional writers. But even as they initiated that process, a problem arose that could have scuttled the whole project.

"A pilot that I'd done earlier for Fox got picked up," Echevarria explains, "and I was obligated to stay with that."

It was a moment that Jeff Wachtel remembers well. "René, Scott, Maira, the USA team and the Viacom team were all gathered in a meeting where we were going to confirm picking up the 'Pilot'," he says. "And suddenly, René got a phone call. He said, 'Excuse me, I have to take this.' He walked out of the meeting..." Wachtel pauses for effect, "...and he *never* came back!" Wachtel laughs at the memory. "We literally had just said, 'Let's do it,' and then we went, 'Wait... wha... where's René?' The next time I saw him was at the premiere party!"

"The timing was terrible," Echevarria admits. Luckily, he already had laid the groundwork for the show's survival by pulling an old friend into the mix.

As showrunner and executive producer of *Star Trek: Deep Space Nine*, Ira Steven Behr had been Echevarria's boss for five years, and the two had developed a lasting friendship. When USA asked for a quick turnaround on the four additional scripts, Echevarria had called Behr with a simple request. "René asked me if I would write *one* episode of a miniseries," Behr reports, "and then hang around for the story breaks on the other three. It sounded like an easy job that would last a couple of weeks, and we'd hang out and have some fun. So I said okay. And literally the next day, René left the show."

Now Behr found himself up against the same dilemmas and deadlines that Echevarria had faced two days earlier. "I was more than a little surprised!" Behr exclaims. But he agreed to step up to the plate. With the onus of building a writing staff on his shoulders, his first decision was to take a chance on someone close at hand.

Craig Sweeny had been René Echevarria's assistant since *Dark Angel*. When he heard that USA wanted additional scripts, the hopeful writer suggested an idea about a serial killer. "René pitched that to USA and they liked it, so I kind of dug my fingers in and hung on for dear life, hoping I'd be allowed to write it," Sweeny says. Now, with Echevarria gone, there was no time for second guessing. "Ira gave me the assignment to write the script that became 'Becoming'," relates Sweeny. "After he saw my first draft, he hired me on-staff."

Behr next turned to Robert Hewitt Wolfe, former executive producer of *Gene*

Above: Breaking into the lair of a suspected serial killer who happens to be a 4400 is just another day at work for NTAC Agents Skouris and Baldwin.

Roddenberry's Andromeda and another veteran of the writing staff from *Deep Space Nine*. Behr offered Wolfe the same deal that Echevarria had offered Behr: one script and assisting in the story breaks. Wolfe accepted, and the writing staff for the miniseries was solid — and very busy. "We had a very difficult mandate," Wolfe recalls, "making the two-hour work all by itself, and the six-hour work all by itself, at the same time making sure the two-hour could lead into the six-hour and the six-hour could lead into a series. The six all had to flow together, and we had to plan alternate endings. It was a challenging way to break a story."

Meanwhile, Peters, Suro and Simon had production concerns to address, starting with finding a location in which to shoot the 'Pilot'. Peters originally had set his story in the desert near San Diego, California, reasoning that it would provide a different setting for the show than the rain forest scenery familiar to audiences of *The X-Files*. "Of course," Peters grins, "I always knew I'd get a phone call saying, 'Change it to the Pacific Northwest, 'cause we're shooting in Vancouver.'"

Economics drove the production north, with the usual financial incentives of shooting in Canada heightened by the availability of sets that Viacom Productions had created in Vancouver for the television series *Jake 2.0*. "It was in a facility that we'd leased there for about eight years," Perry Simon explains. "We'd shot the pilots for *Ed* and *Sabrina, the Teenage Witch* up there."

"*Jake 2.0* was wrapping production, so we moved in," Suro says. "Basically, the only thing we used was a massive, two-story space that, once redressed, became Homeland Security for the first season."

At the same time, the search for actors got underway as the producers set up casting offices in Los Angeles and Vancouver. USA was keen on signing recognizable "names", while the producers hoped to find the absolutely best talent for each role. Word filtered in that Gary Sinise and Sean Bean both were interested in finding television series, and the two rose to the top of the producers' list for the central role of Tom Baldwin.

"We knew that we were a little cable show that wasn't even a series yet. In fact, we were only a two-hour 'Pilot'," Suro admits. "But that also could be a selling point: the actor would only have to commit to six hours. As luck would have it, Joel

Gretsch came in very early on, and we all gravitated to him. He'd recently starred in the highly rated cable miniseries *Taken*, which didn't hurt. And," she adds, "if we'd gotten a name actor and he hadn't wanted to continue, maybe Tom would have died at the end of the six."

For the role of Diana Skouris, the Los Angeles casting team auditioned "many, many" actresses, according to Peters. "But Jacqueline McKenzie owned the room from the second she hit the front door," he recalls. "She was speaking a mile a minute, circling the room like a hummingbird. She had this great quirky quality about her, and was just charming."

The Australian actress was asked to read from scenes that included the character of Maia, Ira Behr points out. "We knew Diana was a woman who is struggling as a parent," he explains. "Many of the other women who came in were interesting and strong, but they didn't have that strange attitude where they're not sure how to deal with kids, and they all talked down to the kids in the audition. With Jacqui, we saw that it was going to be real."

Patrick Flueger was the first actor to try out for the third pivotal character of the show, Shawn Farrell. "In his audition, Patrick was so focused on getting what we were looking for that he scared us," Scott Peters says. "We'd asked him to be a little bit more edgy in one scene, and after he finished he stayed really gruff and growled, 'How's that!! Was I good!?!' After he left, we said, 'Well, he's really good, but I hope he isn't a pain, because he was kind of intense there at the end,'" Peters recalls. "We've laughed about it since, because he's the most kind-hearted guy you could meet."

The fact that one character, Kyle Baldwin, would be unconscious for nearly the entire month of filming the two-hour 'Pilot' presented a unique casting challenge. With little dialogue completed for Kyle, Chad Faust was asked to read lines written for the character of Danny Farrell. "Casting Chad was a Hail Mary Pass," comments Behr, alluding to an American football play in which the ball is passed in desperation with very little chance of success. "In the end, Chad sure as hell caught it."

Four more key characters would fill out the initial cast: returnees Richard Tyler, Lily Moore and Maia Rutledge; and Homeland Security bureau chief, Dennis Ryland.

"We were looking for somebody with name value to play Ryland," Peters recalls. "Jeff Wachtel suggested Peter Coyote. We knew that Peter could seamlessly evolve

NTAC INFORMATION ARCHIVE

"Very soon after I'd begun to develop the show, I came up with the title, *The 4400*," Scott Peters says. "I liked it because it rolled off the tongue. It's like the title *Dances with Wolves* — you have to know what the story is before you understand what it means."

The network, however, didn't agree. "They didn't like the title because their research said that titles with numbers in them do not appeal to women," notes Ira Behr. "So my suggestion was that we should call it '4400 Pairs of Shoes', because then every woman on the planet would tune in."

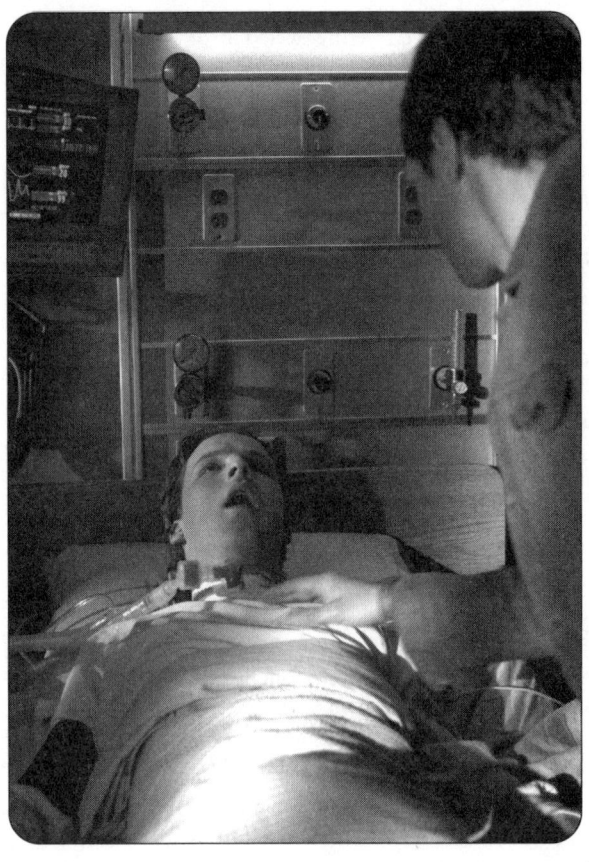

Above: The touch of his cousin Shawn's hand awakens Kyle after three years in a coma.

Ryland from a good guy into a bad guy, and he did exactly what we'd hoped for. He's an actor's actor."

For the role of Richard, Ira Behr had a very specific actor in mind. "I knew he would be too expensive," Behr says cryptically, "but he gave a really nice reading and I *wanted* him in the role." Enter Mahershalalhashbaz Ali — and everything changed. "Ali came in and *was* Richard," says Behr, "this 1950s man. A soft-spoken, kind of conservative, kind of formal guy. You just sensed he was a man outside of his time. And suddenly it didn't matter what I'd wanted before — this was the guy! Ali *won* that role."

"Lily Moore was the hardest character to cast," Suro states. "At the time we were thinking of her as the Virgin Mary, if you will. She needed to have an ethereal quality about her, a purity. And she had to fit with Ali, who we'd already cast." The producers' first choice for the role was Summer Glau. "Summer had an 'out of this world' quality, and is beautiful in such a different kind of way," Suro explains. "But she's *so* young, and we wondered if the age difference with Ali would just be creepy. Ultimately, we decided she was the one, but by then she'd signed to do the movie *Serenity*.

"So we kept looking," Suro continues. "We had to put *some* woman on a plane to Vancouver to start shooting in only five days. Then Laura Allen came in. She had all of that purity, and a more mature quality. And she and Ali were beautiful together. They had great chemistry."

But the producers wouldn't forget Summer Glau. She would show up as mental patient Tess Doerner in the opening episode of season two, and return as a recurring character a season later.

For the youngest character in the ensemble, Maia, they chose Conchita Campbell, who was only eight years old when the 'Pilot' was shot. "The Vancouver casting office sent us a tape of this little girl, and we just went, 'Wow.' She had an intensity about her, and — like Ali — we sensed an 'old soul'. That was perfect,

because she would be playing a character who'd been born in the 1930s. We were really lucky we found Conchita," Suro beams.

The two-hour 'Pilot' of *The 4400* aired on USA Network July 11, 2004, and ranked as the "highest-rated and most-watched new series première on a basic cable network *ever!*" Maira Suro recites proudly.

The night before, at the première party, Suro recalls, "I'd asked Jeff Wachtel how many viewers we needed to have, and he said, 'Anything above three million would be amazing.' The next morning Jeff called me, and all he would say was, 'It's so good. It's so good,' over and over. I had to press him — 'What is it?'" Suro recalls happily. "We'd drawn 7.1 million viewers. That's huge!"

The four subsequent one-hour episodes played through August 8, averaging 6.2 million viewers each, which ranked it as the most watched original cable series of the year, beating out top competitors such as *Nip/Tuck* and *Monk*. At the end of the season, *The 4400* received three Emmy nominations: Outstanding Miniseries; Outstanding Writing; and Cinematography for a Miniseries or Movie. It also was nominated for a Saturn Award for Best Syndicated/Cable Television Series, and a Golden Satellite Award for Best Miniseries. And Conchita Campbell was nominated for a Young Artist Award for Best Performance in a TV Series (Comedy or Drama) — Young Actress Age Ten or Younger. The one winner: the BMI Film and TV Cable Award for music which was shared by the composers of the original songs and soundtracks. ○

Main Cast Credits

> "Four thousand four hundred missing people. The future sent them back in a ball of light. Any of this sound familiar? — **Tom Baldwin 'Life Interrupted'**

SEASONS ONE AND TWO REGULAR CAST:

Tom Baldwin: Joel Gretsch
Diana Skouris: Jacqueline McKenzie
Richard Tyler: Mahershalalhashbaz Ali
Lily Moore Tyler: Laura Allen
Shawn Farrell: Patrick Flueger
Kyle Baldwin: Chad Faust
Danny Farrell: Kaj-Erik Eriksen (season one)
Nikki Hudson: Brooke Nevin (season one)
Dennis Ryland: Peter Coyote (season one)
Nina Jarvis: Samantha Ferris (season two)
Maia Rutledge Skouris: Conchita Campbell (season two)

Pilot

Written by: Scott Peters and René Echevarria

Directed by: Yves Simoneau

Guest Cast: Michael Moriarty (Orson Bailey), Conchita Campbell (Maia Rutledge), Lori Triolo (Linda Baldwin), Chilton Crane (Susan Farrell), Andrew Airlie (Brian Moore), Garwin Sanford (Adam Kensington)

Federal agent Tom Baldwin's twenty-year-old son Kyle has been in a coma for three years. Kyle was found lying unconscious on Highland Beach the same night that his cousin Shawn Farrell disappeared. Convinced there was a connection, Tom took a leave of absence from his job to search for Shawn, an obsession that drove a wedge between him and his wife Linda.

Life on Earth is about to change. Scientists report a comet is headed for the planet. At the Seattle Department of Homeland Security (Home Sec), Tom's former boss Dennis Ryland and his agents are startled when the "comet" slows for a landing! Agent Diana Skouris heads for the touchdown point and watches as a ball of light approaches and then suddenly explodes. When the haze clears, Diana sees that thousands of men, women and children have appeared before her.

Home Sec rounds up all 4400 people — each of whom disappeared within the past sixty years. Knowing that Shawn Farrell is one of the "returnees", Tom asks Ryland to reinstate him. Ryland agrees, partnering him with Diana. The team quickly learns that none of the returnees remember anything about their time away. Tom is bitterly disappointed when Shawn claims to know nothing about how Kyle was injured.

After the 4400 are released from quarantine, many find there's nowhere to go. Eight-year-old Maia Rutledge disappeared sixty years ago; no one's waiting for her, so she's sent to live with foster parents. Richard Tyler, a black fighter pilot who vanished during the Korean War, has no home to return to. However, his sense of isolation is eased by his friendship with fellow detainee Lily Moore, who bears an astonishing resemblance to Richard's former lover — Lily's long dead grandmother!

During Lily's absence, her husband Brian remarried. Their eleven-year-old daughter Heidi believes his current wife is her mother, and Brian doesn't want to destroy that illusion. Distraught, Lily discovers she's pregnant — although she wasn't before she disappeared. Feeling alone, she's relieved when Richard approaches her. The two decide to face their new lives together.

Returnee Orson Bailey learns that his beloved wife is in a nursing home, and his company belongs to his deceased partner's son, Adam Kensington. Orson tries to get his old position back, but Kensington turns him away. Later, Orson goes to Kensington's home, but Kensington refuses to open his front gate, and as Orson shakes the barricade in rage, the lavish house trembles. Inside, Kensington collapses and dies of multiple skull fractures. The police question Bailey, but there's no way to prove he was involved.

Shawn has a difficult time readjusting to high school life. The students call him a freak, and Brad, a classmate with a score to settle, bullies him. Even Shawn's brother Danny feels uneasy around him. Only Danny's girlfriend Nikki is happy

about his return.

Maia's foster parents, unnerved when they realize she has the ability to see future events, return her to the quarantine facility.

Shawn, too, has developed some odd abilities. He brings a dead bird back to life just by touching it. Then at school, after Brad initiates a fight, Shawn discovers he has the power to drain the life from his nemesis.

Feeling that Bailey may be a danger to himself and the community, Tom and Diana try to bring him in, but they're bombarded by his out-of-control emotions. Finally, Diana shoots the returnee, saving her and Tom from Kensington's gruesome fate.

Depressed, Shawn visits Kyle. As he stares at his cousin's unconscious form, he places a hand on Kyle's chest. Kyle suddenly begins to gasp and stir. Alarmed, Shawn removes his hand, and Kyle slumps back into his coma, leaving Shawn wondering what he just did.

> "So between you and me, what do you think happened to them? Where do you think they've been?" - Tom

Ensconced in the upper floors of a high rise office building, executive producer Ira Steven Behr and his fellow writers, Robert Hewitt Wolfe and Craig Sweeny, faced the

Above: Dennis Ryland (Peter Coyote) quizzes Tom and Diana about a returnee who seems to have developed unusual abilities.

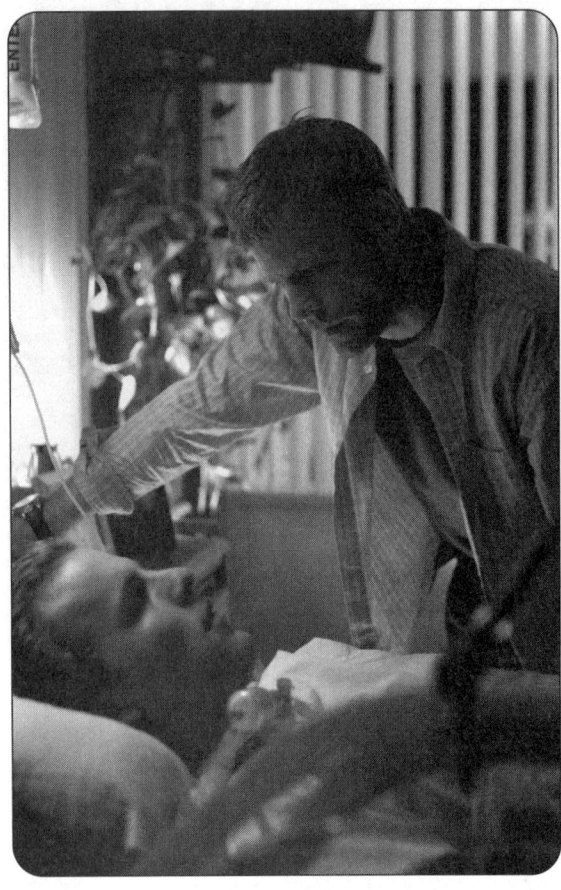

task of revising a two-hour script titled, simply, 'Pilot', while simultaneously creating four additional one-hour scripts. From far below, where Wilshire and Westwood Boulevards create one of Los Angeles' busiest corners, the assault of automotive din rose as a constant distraction from the task at hand. And in the building itself — another distraction.

"My office door had a little clear strip of glass in it," Behr says, "and a few times every day I'd look up to see a pair of eyes, like the eyes and glasses in *The Great Gatsby*, staring at me." When Behr's own eyes happened to meet those of the curious onlookers — generally executives from the business side of Viacom Studios — the door would open and "They'd come in, stand in front of my desk and say, 'How's the script going?'" Behr recalls. "I wanted to say, 'Fine, *until you interrupted!*'"

Being a gentleman, Behr suppressed his ire. But when he mentioned the distraction at home, his wife Laura came up with a bold solution. "Why don't you blue your beard?" she stated, and the writer recognized her wisdom. The next morning when Behr arrived in the building, the facial hair that he'd worn for years now glowed a radiant blue. "It freaked everyone out," Behr laughs. The ploy served to stop people from opening the door; however, Behr sighs, "The eyes didn't stop."

Above: Even though he hadn't been the best father, Tom sits with his son every day while Kyle is in a coma.

At the time, the 'Pilot' script bore little resemblance to the one that would go into production in a matter of weeks. Rather than presenting a series of abductions that introduce key 4400 members, it opened with Homeland Security agent Tom Racker being awakened by a phone call and ordered to the office; next a group of agents discuss an "object". "It's not a comet or an asteroid, or anything else that we know

NTAC INFORMATION ARCHIVE

Scott Peters had a very specific reason for clustering the 4400 abductions within the past sixty years. "We didn't want to do stories about Ogg the Caveman coming back with a club," he says. "Or Elizabethan costume dramas either. We wanted to stay as relevant as possible."

of," boss agent Ryland Cook insists. After pages of discussion about such things as warning the public to "tape their windows", the mysterious object delivers... "People. Thousands. Naked as the day they were born." Among those naked people: Tom's missing nephew, Leith.

USA Network's arrangement with the producers required that the four follow up scripts be approved by the time principal photography on the 'Pilot' was completed. As they geared up for shooting, "We were working on all the scripts at once, hitting them all every day," Behr notes. "Then Robert had to leave, and it was just Craig and me. Finally, Craig and I moved into a production trailer in Vancouver. We'd get network notes about this scene and that scene, until sometimes we couldn't remember which episode we were talking about," Behr says with what appears to be a smile — although he might be gritting his teeth. "It was quite a grueling experience."

Above: The 4400 people who are returned to Highland Beach have no memory of where they've been — or even of having been gone.

The move to the trailer wasn't Behr's first trip to Vancouver for the project. He and fellow executive producers Scott Peters and Maira Suro had traveled north numerous times to scout locations with director Yves Simoneau, veteran of dozens of movies and television shows, including *Amelia Earhart: The Final Flight*, and *44 Minutes: The North Hollywood Shoot-Out*.

"Yves had always been my choice for director," says Suro. "I'd talked to him a year earlier while we were developing this with Fox Television. When we got the green light at USA, my first phone call was to Yves. I said, 'Hi, I'm that person who called you a year ago.' He jumped in and became a fantastic partner."

One of Simoneau's goals was to establish a visual style for the show that could readily be continued by other directors in future episodes — and he knew exactly how to do that. "The most important thing was to plant all of the characters very realistically," he states in a lilting Quebecer accent. "We put those characters in a realistic environment, and then treated that environment in a slightly surreal way. For instance, when Tom and Diana are going through Orson Bailey's belongings, we

Above: Decorated Air Force pilot Richard Tyler is transported from an era when prejudice was based solely on skin color to one where it's based on fear of the unknown.

shot from under a glass table. It's an unusual way of looking at things, but the viewer wouldn't say, 'This isn't possible.' They'd just find it unsettling. It's looking at reality in an acute way."

Adding to that unsettling effect, the director chose long lenses to shoot very tight shots, and wide lenses to shoot close-ups. "The lenses bring the décor close to the actors, or push the décor away from the actors to isolate them in space," he says.

"Yves gave us a world with great scope," Suro enthuses. "And he inserted those extreme close-ups to show how the character within that big world was feeling."

That stylistic approach, Simoneau knew, would be easily applicable by subsequent directors on the show that, he says, "will go on for a long, long time, because it offers 4400 stories."

Principal photography for *The 4400* rolled at an exterior location on the shore of Bunsen Lake outside of Vancouver. Mother Nature, however, presented the filmmakers with an inauspicious start. "It rained for five days," Scott Peters says with a resigned sigh. "The opening sequence was supposed to be a sunny day with Maia and her family having a lovely picnic."

"It was pouring rain that day," Conchita Campbell, who plays Maia, confirms, "and I was *so* cold."

With no time to wait for the weather to improve, Simoneau reminded Peters that they had to shoot something that day, "So I rewrote the scene on the spot," the show's creator says. "Now the picnic takes place in a car." With rain falling hard during the scene, the actors' dialogue was unusable, so they had to rerecord it several weeks later, on a "looping" stage.

Despite the spontaneous changes, Conchita Campbell, eight years old at the time,

NTAC INFORMATION ARCHIVE

During the 'Pilot', a talk show host named Barbara Yates is briefly seen on a TV monitor by Maia and Orson Bailey. When the writers decided to turn Yates' character into a personal adversary for Ryland in two subsequent episodes, they recast the role with accomplished Canadian actor Helen Shaver, who already had been assigned to helm 'The New and Improved Carl Morrissey'.

took it all in stride. "In the one scene I did outside," she says, "it was pouring, and while I was walking, the ground went down a bit, and I slipped and fell. Everyone thought that I got hurt, but then I lifted my face up and they saw that I was laughing like crazy," she adds, still smiling. "That was pretty funny."

"This being Vancouver, it rains constantly, so you just shoot in the rain," production designer Steve Geaghan points out. "The best way to do that is to ignore it, and if you don't light it you won't see it. Just keep the actors dry and stop them from blinking if the raindrops hit their face and hair, and the audience is never the wiser." But even that sage advice almost didn't work the following day.

"We went to shoot the interior of the tent where Richard gets hit by the other soldier, and the floor of the tent was underwater. We had to put plywood down," Peters notes. "So when you see Richard get struck, he collapses, but he doesn't actually touch the ground, because Ali slid down that tent's pole and then stayed in a crouched position. If he'd actually sat, he'd have gotten soaking wet and he would have had to change wardrobe constantly. But actually," Peters concludes, "that worked out. Ali made it look as if Richard wasn't going to go down for those guys. It's terrific when real life logistics combine with something that works for the scene."

One real life situation didn't help the scene at all, yet the entire cast and crew remembers it fondly — especially Joel Gretsch. "It was my very first scene working with Chad Faust," Gretsch recalls. "I was giving this little telephone speech to Tom's sister, saying, "The comet is coming. I love you, sis." And on the first take, Chad started to *snore* in the background. I thought, 'What the hell is that noise!' That was my introduction to Chad!"

"I knew that I'd be spending the day laying in bed as if I was in a coma," Chad Faust explains. "And I didn't want to be fully rested, laying in bed and trying to be still, so I stayed up the night before. While Joel was in the middle of his emotional close-up, I actually fell asleep. When I woke up, I felt terrible," the actor says with a grin. "It became one of those legendary moments: 'The Kid Snores'."

Although Tom Baldwin was personally connected to the returnees through his son and nephew, his partner, Diana Skouris, initially saw them only from a scientific/law enforcement point of view — until she was forced into a very intimate interaction: shooting Orson Bailey. The scene is tragic, and understandably horrific for Diana who had never shot anyone before. But on the set, that inexperience brought about an entirely different set of emotions. "I'm not experienced using a gun," Jaqueline McKenzie, the actress who portrays Diana, says. "So while I thought I was aiming my gun toward Michael Moriarty's chest, apparently the tip of the barrel was trained very carefully on his testicles. I was saying, 'Orson — stop it now,' and Yves Simoneau and his crew were all in stitches." ○

The New & Improved Carl Morrissey

Written by: Ira Steven Behr
Directed by: Helen Shaver

Guest Cast: David Eigenberg (Carl Morrissey), Conchita Campbell (Maia Rutledge), Lori Triolo (Linda Baldwin), Andrew Airlie (Brian Moore), Kathleen Wilhoite (Grace Morrissey)

Returnee Carl Morrissey hates how much his old neighborhood deteriorated while he was gone. Ignoring his wife Grace's warning about how dangerous Bradley Park has become, Carl enters his old haunt and is attacked by muggers. But he surprises both the thugs and himself by responding with almost supernatural speed and strength. Carl reasons that whoever took the 4400 must have changed them with some purpose in mind — and now he knows what *his* purpose is.

At Seattle Home Sec, Ryland discusses Maia Rutledge's precognitive abilities with Tom and Diana. Although Maia's powers frighten others, Diana feels sympathy for the eight-year-old. Still, she's startled when Maia asks to come home with her.

Kyle's doctor informs Tom that his son experienced a spike in brain activity the night that Shawn paid him a visit. Shawn, however, stubbornly denies that he did anything.

As Richard and Lily hunt for an apartment, Lily realizes she can tell what her unborn child is thinking, and that the baby perceives things outside of the womb. Whenever it doesn't like what's happening, the baby makes Lily feel physically ill.

Hearing about a vigilante crime fighter that might be a 4400, Tom and Diana investigate. Grace leads them to Bradley Park, where they find Carl, mortally wounded. He's rid the place of graffiti, but he's been stabbed. As he dies in Grace's arms, the agents wonder why Carl was given special powers, only to be killed when he used them. Then they learn that Carl's community, inspired by his efforts, has united to clean up the neighborhood. Could this be what was intended?

Diana decides to become Maia's foster parent, while Tom's child takes a turn for the worse. When Shawn shows up at the hospital, Tom eyes him, wondering if his nephew is responsible for Kyle's downturn. Guilt-ridden, Shawn can't help wondering the same thing.

> "This is what I was meant to do. This is my destiny." - Carl

One of the first decisions the show's producers had to make concerned the various abilities that the 4400 would develop. Everyone quickly came to an agreement that they should seem rooted in reality, rather than magic or comic book lore.

"We did not use the word 'powers'," emphasizes Ira Behr. "We shouted at people who came to the office and used that word, 'They're abilities! No one's wearing a latex costume!'"

And yet the title character of the first one-hour episode came very close to crossing that line. In fact, Scott Peters felt that he leaped over it in a single bound. "Carl Morrissey seemed a lot like a super hero to me," he says. "His ability took the

show away from the grounded perspective that we'd started with."

But while Morrissey's discovery that he had the fighting prowess of, if not a super hero, then at the very least a martial arts superstar of Bruce Lee or Jet Li's caliber, he still had that core of normalcy that allowed the audience to identify with him.

"Carl just wanted to make the neighborhood safe for his wife," says Maira Suro. "Yeah, he gets caught up in it after a while, but it didn't start with, 'I'm going to use my ability to get in the newspaper.' He wanted to take care of the neighborhood because he loved his wife and all of his history was in that neighborhood."

Ironically, it hadn't started out that way.

"My first draft had a lot of humor in it," Behr says. "Carl Morrissey came back the same loser that he'd been when he was abducted. But he had an odd ability, and his wife wanted him to make money off of it. They had an entirely different relationship," recalls Behr, "but nobody liked it, so we had to refit the whole episode."

Above: Grace (Kathleen Wilhoite) admits that she's worried her husband's new abilities may bring him to harm.

NTAC INFORMATION ARCHIVE

Ira Behr and David Eigenberg had never met prior to the filming of 'The New and Improved Carl Morrissey', but later they became good friends. "We kept bumping into each other. I mean, if he was stalking me, then it's creepy. But I think it was just a little bit of kismet," Eigenberg quips.

Above: Maia's isolation touches a chord in Diana.

That's when the writing team struck on the idea of Carl realizing that "he isn't the loser, it's his home environment that has become the loser. So he decides that he can make it better," Behr says.

"That made it more interesting," adds Suro. "I think that's why we got such a big tune-in number on the miniseries, because women were part of the audience. Women don't typically gravitate to sci-fi, but we'd created a show with characters like Carl, who were real and feeling and relatable."

In the end, the character's ability brought him to a tragic end, dying on the same park bench where he'd once proposed to his wife. "We could have done more with Carl," Behr says. "I'm sorry that we killed him. But we were looking for punchy episodes, so we had to do it. His death scene had some poignancy to it."

However, according to David Eigenberg, the actor who played Carl, "The best part of it for me was that he *did* die, because we can't live in a society where you just go out on your own and become the judge and jury if things go bad."

Although he disagreed with Carl's vigilante bent, the actor found a personal way to connect with the character. "The only way that violence makes sense to me is if it's laden with pathos," Eigenberg explains. "If Carl had been doing this just out of blind ambition, then he'd have been an idiot. The violence had to show a sadness too."

Two very important elements were established in the episode. The first was the "theory room", which emerged because of an ongoing series of notes from

NTAC INFORMATION ARCHIVE

"For the first couple of episodes, Chad Faust showed up at all the read-throughs, even though his role was to lay there unconscious," Scott Peters reports. "That told us a lot about who Chad is, as well as the kind of actor he is."

"Everyone kept saying that they were very impressed that the coma kid was coming to table reads," Faust says. "But I was just stoked on the idea of having this family unit, and I wanted to be a part of it. I came to everything."

USA. "They said, 'We need summation scenes!'" Behr says with a sigh. "They wanted us to stop the action and have Tom and Diana stand around on street corners and theorize. So we gave them the theory room!"

Suro briefly worried that the writers' "on-the-nose" response to the network's request might make the executives think the writers were taunting them. But Behr convinced her otherwise. "I told her that they'd like it, because it gave us a chance — without stopping the action — to create a really quirky character inside Homeland Security who isn't an agent running around trying to kill people."

That character, of course, was Marco Pacella, played by Richard Kahan, whose role would take on additional weight as the show progressed. Judging by the response on USA's official bulletin board for the series, Marco received a thumbs-up from the show's fanbase. As for the theory room itself, USA's Jeff Wachtel found it the perfect setting for what he calls, "a nice ground level way to keep the audience informed."

The other important element established in 'The New and Improved Carl Morrissey' was the loving relationship between Richard and Lily. "We had our first kiss," recalls Laura Allen, who plays Lily. "Which we didn't rehearse," she adds.

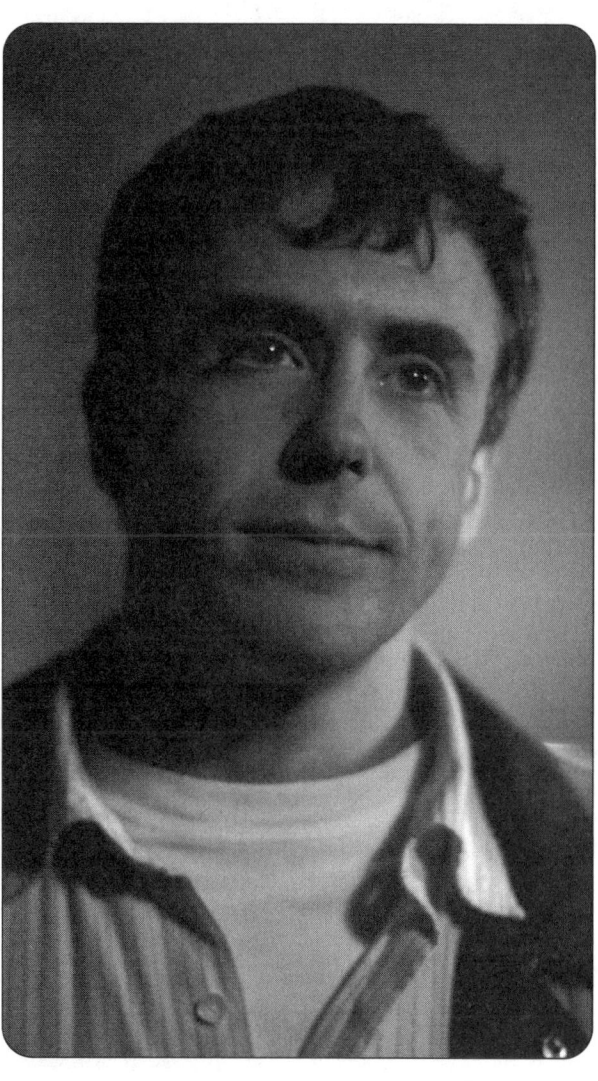

"Lily and Richard were so connected by their experiences that they had feelings for each other in spite of each other."

"They had a sense of family from the beginning," actor Mahershalalhashbaz Ali agrees. "Richard was surprised when Lily said that the apartment was for both of them, but if you slow down and allow yourself to let the scene seep into your heart, you see that it has elements that are really to be appreciated. That's why I think this series is really special." ○

Above: Carl Morrissey (David Eigenberg) gets carried away with his new abilities — and suffers the consequences.

Becoming

Written by: Craig Sweeny
Directed by: David Straiton

Guest Cast: Billy Campbell (Jordan Collier), Lee Tergesen (Oliver Knox), Conchita Campbell (Maia Rutledge), Lori Triolo (Linda Baldwin), Peter Lacroix (Jim Conrad), Helen Shaver (Barbara Yates)

Fanned by the broadcasts of muckraker Barbara Yates, public unease grows over the 4400's odd abilities. Well-known hotel magnate Jordan Collier decides to "out" himself in order to give a human face to the demonized returnees.

At Home Sec, Ryland worries about a situation that could increase public antagonism. Oliver Knox, believed responsible for a string of murders in Friday Harbor twenty-one years before, is a 4400. Now that he's returned, another woman has been killed. Coincidence?

In Friday Harbor, Tom and Diana learn Knox has an alibi for the time of the recent death, then discover evidence that someone else may be responsible. By the time they find the other man, he's killed himself, leaving behind a note confessing to the murders.

Back in Seattle, Collier invites the 4400s to gather for a group support session. When he learns Lily is pregnant, Jordan takes a special interest in her and offers Richard a security job at his foundation.

Shawn, troubled by Kyle's worsening condition, tries to remember what happened that night on Highland Beach. At last he recalls that the white light that took him away *actually was meant for Kyle*. When Shawn tried to free Kyle from the mysterious beam, he was taken instead, leaving Kyle behind, comatose.

Another woman is murdered. A blood-drenched killer confesses to all of the slayings, despite the fact that he's too young to have committed the earlier ones. Later, Tom and Diana foil an attempt to kill a woman named Felicia. Seeing surveillance photos of her would-be assailant speaking to Knox prior to the attack, the agents wonder if the returnee has the ability to talk others into killing for him. But before they can question him, Knox goes after Felicia himself. The agents apprehend him just in time, and the serial killer is imprisoned in a soundproofed cell.

Returning to Seattle, Tom finds Shawn in Kyle's hospital room. To his profound amazement, he finds his son awake, apparently healed.

NTAC INFORMATION ARCHIVE

When Tom Baldwin apprehends serial killer Oliver Knox in 'Becoming', the script calls for Tom to "backhand Knox across the face with the barrel of his gun." Prior to shooting the scene, Joel Gretsch and Lee Tergesen rehearsed the move with the stunt coordinators; but as they filmed it, Tergesen and Gretsch were standing too close together, and Gretsch's prop gun brushed the other actor's face. The accident dismayed Gretsch as much as it pained Tergesen. It was a Friday, the day the crew joins in a weekly Five Dollar Draw game. At the end of the day, to Gretsch's surprise, he won the pot — and immediately handed his winnings to his 'victim'.

"How long have I been in the dark?" - Kyle

"People already have a notion in their heads about what a character looks like before he shows up," Billy Campbell says. "And if you show up looking different, it's a jolt." Which explains the turmoil that arose when the recently cast actor arrived to portray Jordan Collier for the first time.

"We were getting ready to shoot the scene where a group of returnees gathers at the lake where they'd all landed, and Billy

showed up at the location with a beard," Scott Peters explains. "So Ira and I introduced ourselves and then said, tentatively, 'By the way, you're not married to the beard, are you?' And Billy answered, 'Oh, there's no way I can shave my beard.' He said that he'd need it for an upcoming role. And Ira and I just looked at each other and said, 'Uh, oh.'"

Jordan Collier had been conceived in the writers' room as "a character that could unite the 4400," Behr explains. "We had the idea of a powerful man with a messiah complex who actually might *be* the messiah. One of the first names that came up when we started to discuss actors was Billy Campbell." To say that Behr was excited at the prospect is an understatement. "I thought, 'Oh, baby!'" he recalls with a grin.

Behr wasn't alone in his enthusiasm. Everyone at the network, the studio and in the producers offices liked the idea of working with Campbell. "Billy is a character actor trapped in a leading man's body," Scott Peters says. "He has great instincts for playing things off the main track."

But no one had expected that beard. "He's a handsome guy!" USA's Jackie de Crinis says. "You want to see that face."

Above: When Jordan Collier (Billy Campbell) discovers that Lily is pregnant, he begins to orchestrate a plan to control the baby's life.

Above: The agents visit with Friday Harbor's Sheriff Jim Conrad (Peter Lacroix) when a serial killer reappears after more than two decades.

Now, on his first day of shooting, the unexpected issue of Campbell's facial hair had to be discussed with all the powers that be. Unfortunately, the remoteness of the location meant that no one could get a cell phone signal. "We were up in Whoville," Behr sighs. "I caught a ride down the mountain to a clearing, where I could get reception. And there I was, standing alone in the middle of nowhere, without a car, not knowing where I was — and no one I called answered the phone!" Eventually contact was achieved, and after several discussions between Los Angeles and Vancouver, a determination was made that both Campbell and his beard would stay.

NTAC INFORMATION ARCHIVE

"I originally gave Patrick Flueger's character the name Leith," Scott Peters says. "We changed it, but then Patrick was incensed because he loved the name. He came into my office and said, 'What can I do to have you change the name back?' I told him, 'It's not me, I love the name too, but...'"

Comments Ira Behr, "Thank God, sometimes the names don't clear."

And what had Campbell been doing throughout the crisis? "I didn't want to seem confrontational or aloof, so I sat in a chair out in the parking lot reading a book," he says with a smile.

While Jordan Collier was destined to play an important role in *The 4400*, the character wasn't the focus of his first episode. That position fell to serial killer Oliver Knox, played by Lee Tergesen. Craig Sweeny had come up with the Knox story after hearing news coverage of 'The Green River Killer', a man who later admitted to killing forty-eight women in the Seattle area between 1982 and 1998. "He hadn't been captured," Sweeny says, "he had simply stopped killing, and you had to wonder why. It seemed quite organic that he could have been abducted by whoever took the 4400. After mulling over what his ability would be, we thought of mind control, and that worked into those creepy whispering scenes."

The episode gave the audience another dose of Marco Pacella and the theory room, as he first discusses the concept of the "ripple effect". "Marco's job, which is my job, is to deliver information," actor Richard Kahan says, "so I am the definition of exposition. But the writers have done a good job of giving life to this character."

Above: Jordan Collier: hero, villain... or a little of each?

A critical bit of information was revealed to the audience in this, the middle episode of the miniseries. 'Becoming' explained why Shawn Farrell had been abducted while his cousin Kyle Baldwin had been left in a coma. The sequence actually had been shot for the 'Pilot', but, Sweeny says, "we held it back because we didn't want to reveal that much so soon."

The episode ends as the arc of one character begins. Following his recollection that it was *his* intervention that caused Kyle's injury, Shawn goes to the hospital in hopes that he can use his ability to awaken Kyle. Chad Faust, having spent the majority of his scenes up to that point silently lying on his back, appreciated the opportunity to finally deliver a line of dialogue in something other than a flashback. "How long was I in the dark?" Faust recites from memory. "When I read that line in the script, I could see that Kyle was going to become a really interesting character for me to play. That line was perfect." ◯

Trial By Fire

Written by: Robert Hewitt Wolfe
Directed by: Nick Gomez

Guest Cast: Billy Campbell (Jordan Collier), Mark Valley (Warren Lytell), Conchita Campbell (Maia Rutledge), Lori Triolo (Linda Baldwin), Michael Eklund (Dean Keating), Shane Meier (Glen Keating), Helen Shaver (Barbara Yates)

Tom and Linda are unprepared for how disoriented Kyle seems once he's home. He recognizes the faces of relatives and friends but claims he doesn't *know* them, and obsessively searches for clues to something, but can't explain what or why.

When a list of the 4400's names and addresses hits the Internet, Ryland believes Barbara Yates is responsible for the leak *and* its repercussions; someone is targeting returnees' residences with pipe bombs. After Richard and Lily's apartment is bombed, Collier offers them a home in the gated community he's purchased, claiming he wants to provide a safe haven for returnees.

Tom thanks Shawn for healing Kyle, and suggests they find out more about his ability. Shawn declines, saying he already feels like an outcast. Only Nikki remains close, and as her attraction to Shawn grows, she breaks up with his brother Danny. Not long after, she and Shawn give in to their feelings and make love.

Marco Pacella, who heads up Home Sec's theory room, believes each case that Tom and Diana investigate has a ripple effect. Orson Bailey's murder of Kensington saved defrauded investors from financial ruin. Carl Morrissey's escapades inspired a community to reclaim its neighborhood. Perhaps the actions of returnee Oliver Knox triggered the current rash of bombings. Pursuing that rationale, the agents track down and capture two brothers who want to avenge their sister, whom Knox murdered. The ripple effect? The bombings have changed the public's perception of the 4400 from potential threat to sympathetic victims.

Just as Ryland digs up information about Barbara Yates that guarantees her smear campaign against the 4400 will cease, Agent Warren Lytell arrives from Home Sec headquarters to "help" Ryland clean up the "mess" surrounding his oversight of the 4400. Lytell is especially disturbed by the relationships Tom and Diana have with Shawn and Maia, which he sees as conflicts of interest. Lytell is also curious about Kyle, who's just made a startling confession to his father: *he's not really Kyle.*

NTAC INFORMATION ARCHIVE

"When Joel and I jumped out of the helicopter in 'Trial By Fire', I found that I couldn't run while ducking the blade and holding the damn gun out in front of my face," Jacqueline McKenzie says. "You'd have to be a Cossack dancer to do it. When I leapt out of the door, I was so frightened of being decapitated that I did a skootch maneuver like a dog in the park. And when they called, 'Cut,' I saw that the entire crew was just rolling with laughter. I thought, 'Well, that's just bloody great, I've got great credibility now.'"

> **"Someone's coming who'll make everything better. We just have to wait a little longer." - Maia**

Generally, by the time shooting starts on the fifth hour of a series, an actor has a grasp on who his character is. But for the actor playing former "coma kid" Kyle Baldwin, 'Trial By Fire' represented a challenge. The newly awakened Kyle was coming home from the hospital. It was the first time he'd be able to interact with family and friends. Yet the script indicated Kyle was unable to connect with anything or anyone — and Chad Faust was

having a tough time translating that behavior to his performance.

"After I got the script, I went to my hotel room and tried to figure out how to approach it," Faust says. "I kept thinking, 'Who is this kid?' I started moving around, pacing, and then I actually began rearranging the furniture in the room, putting some of it upside-down and stacking it. And eventually I realized that *this*, pacing and moving stuff, trying to figure out who he is, would be what *he'd* do in his situation. So I brought that to the screen."

Call it method acting. Or at least, method furniture moving.

Joel Gretsch already had a handle on who Tom Baldwin was by this time, at least in terms of his job-related behavior. But Kyle's identity crisis required him to find different levels of Tom's personality as the worried father tried to keep it together, for his own sake and his son's. "Tom wanted to look for moments of normalcy," Gretsch explains. "And they came in increments. When Kyle woke up, Tom thought, 'Oh, thank god, I've got him back.' Then he went to, 'Okay, how *cognitive* is he?' Well, he's in a fog, but he's alive. So next it was 'Okay, I'm taking him home' and 'Okay, now that we're in the house…'" At each step, Gretsch pitched his performance in a slightly different key. "I played it one increment at a time," he reports.

Above: Agents Skouris and Baldwin arrest the Keating brothers after they launch a killing spree against innocent 4400s.

Unfortunately, bringing Kyle to the formerly familiar setting only served to confuse him more. He expressed his frustration physically, knocking things off shelves and ripping apart family photos. Once again Faust turned to method techniques, drawing on personal emotions and memories to shape his performance. He brought in a family album, allowing the set decorating department to duplicate the photos. They then shuffled the dupes into the pile, along with images of people Faust didn't know. "That was cool," Faust says, "because when we shot the scene of Kyle going through the snapshots, I let myself follow the reality. There I was ripping up a picture of my brother, tearing his face in half, or one of my aunts holding me as a child. And in between I'd hit these other photos of people I didn't recognize at all. It helped to shape my frame of mind."

For the scene in which Kyle sits naked under the sprinklers, a lot less "method" was required. "It was early spring in Vancouver, and the water was so cold that I was shivering between takes," Faust groans. "But Kyle wasn't supposed to feel *anything*, so every time they called 'Action' I had to just suck it up and stop shaking."

Because the scene called for Kyle to be "in the buff", wardrobe provided him with a dancer's belt. "It makes it look like you're naked, but you're covered," he says. "But

NTAC INFORMATION ARCHIVE

"Here's the thing. The ripple effect worked, but it became such a crutch that the network wanted it in every episode," Ira Behr explains. "But we don't like to do the same thing every week, so after a while, we got bored with the ripple effect. I guess there were some fans who wanted to know 'What happened to the ripple effect?' Well, so many things have happened, and time has passed, and you have to remember, all we are seeing is one ripple of the effect. You can't say that's definitely *the* ripple effect, because *that* will have a ripple effect — that's why it's called a ripple effect. So it was all made a little bit with spit and polish and a wink and a nudge. We knew it was done for that reason, but enough is enough." Behr pauses, then concludes, "But you never know, you might hear the words 'ripple effect' again."

it kept slipping so the camera could see it. Eventually I just tore it off and did the scene butt naked!"

The episode provided defining moments for other cast members as well. Laura Allen's Lily found herself growing increasingly paranoid over Collier's interest in her. "It started to feel like *Rosemary's Baby*," admits Allen. "I became very defensive and protective," she continues, slipping into her 4400 persona. "There was such an interest in my baby, in my body. Collier kept offering Richard and I things and we kept taking them, until I began to wonder if he had ulterior motives."

For Mahershalalhashbaz Ali, 'Trial By Fire' was an important footnote to what he calls "the journey of Richard". "Every time he starts to get a little comfortable — and I suspect this was true even before he got abducted — something happens," explains Ali. "He and Lily's grandmother were about to start a family, and then *ping*! He gets beat up, and then the next thing he knows there's this big ball of light! Then he and Lily start to live a comfortable life together, but people expose their names on TV, and there's the bomb. He just wants peace. But I don't think Richard's ever truly comfortable. That's the engine for his character."

The revelation of the returnees' names and addresses provided some nice fodder for Peter Coyote's Dennis Ryland when he decides to permanently rid himself of talk show host Barbara Yates, who he blames for the leak. The scene where he confronts Yates in the limo, notes Ira Behr, "shows just how tough Ryland is. He's ruthless."

"Well, yeah," agrees Coyote. "He's a tough guy. You don't put creampuffs in jobs where you have to look after public safety." But public safety can be a double-edged sword. "We want them to protect us, but then we get quite cranky about the things they have to do," he muses. "I try to get that ambivalence in Ryland, because the same qualities that make him good at protecting people *can* go awry, so that he'll suddenly take on a unilateral anti-civil libertarian position." Which is essentially the direction the writers would set him in season two.

But was Ryland right about Yates? While the script implies that Yates outed the whereabouts of the 4400, Billy Campbell has his own theory. "I think there's a distinct probability that Collier was the one leaking the information," he reveals, "just so he could get the whole group of them under his wing at his new housing community." ○

Above: Her unborn baby's ability to communicate with her mother isn't always a pleasant experience for Lily.

Opposite: Richard's military training makes him an able head of security at Collier's gated community.

White Light

Written by: Scott Peters
Directed by: Tim Hunter

Guest Cast: Billy Campbell (Jordan Collier), Mark Valley (Warren Lytell), Conchita Campbell (Maia Rutledge), Lori Triolo (Linda Baldwin), Chilton Crane (Susan Farrell)

After Tom and Linda take Kyle to the hospital, Lytell removes him to a secret location for testing. Lily and Richard learn that Collier has kept under wraps the possibility that Richard might be the baby's father, presumably because it would bring the couple closer. When Collier delivers disquieting information to Lily about Richard's past, it seems to confirm that he's trying to split them up. The couple packs their bags.

At Home Sec, Tom threatens to shoot Lytell, but Ryland promises to help Tom find Kyle through official channels. However, with Marco's covert assistance, Diana and Tom figure out the location and successfully liberate Kyle. The boy insists they take him to Highland Beach and Tom complies, although he's worried that Lytell and Ryland will catch up with them.

Nikki reveals her relationship with Shawn to Danny, who confronts his brother. Fending Danny off, Shawn inadvertently begins to drain his brother of life. Their stunned mother intervenes and Shawn flees.

Collier intercepts Richard and Lily as they're about to depart, saying that only he can protect Lily's baby. When Collier grabs Lily, he's assaulted by a powerful blast of energy from the baby, giving the couple an opportunity to escape. That night, Shawn asks Collier for refuge.

At Highland Beach, Tom is startled when Kyle begins to glow. As Lytell and Ryland move in, Tom reaches out to the boy, and is suffused in white light…

Suddenly he and Kyle are in their own private reality. Kyle explains that he's actually a being from Earth's future. His people abducted and changed the 4400 in order to prevent a catastrophe that will leave humanity on the verge of extinction. Kyle was *supposed* to be taken so he could serve as a channel, guiding Tom through his dealings with the returnees. But Shawn's attempt to save Kyle changed everything…

Diana and the other agents hear nothing of this conversation. Frozen within a circle of light, it appears to them that Tom is about to be abducted. Diana attempts to pull Tom out, but is repelled by an energy field. Lytell reacts by putting a bullet in Kyle.

The light disappears, and Kyle collapses. Tom cradles his son as the boy dies… but seconds later, the area is filled with blinding flashes. When the light dissipates, Kyle's wound is gone. He's alive! To Kyle, not a day has passed since he and Shawn sat together on the beach. For Tom, it's the beginning of a whole new life.

> "Kyle was meant to be a channel - a way to communicate with you, to guide you in your dealings with the returnees. But something went wrong." - Future Kyle

"After we'd premiered, the press kept asking, 'When are you going to show an alien?'" Maira Suro laughs. "But our people hadn't been abducted by aliens, and we

Above: Tom Baldwin receives a private message from "future Kyle".

didn't want to spill the beans on that."

Suro and her partners recognized early that keeping the abductors' identity a secret was good strategy. In fact, they'd used it as the capper to their pitch to the USA network executives, with René Echevarria describing the climactic scene between Tom and Kyle before dramatically delivering the big reveal, "We're just like you — we're future humans." That revelation did the trick. USA was in.

But although the producers and writers knew that the show would best be served if that secret were kept for a long time, no one knew how long they would be in production. "In case we didn't get picked up for a second season, we needed some resolution," USA's Jackie de Crinis explains. And so a decision was made. The abductors would be revealed at the end of the miniseries — which caused Ira Behr great consternation. "I said, 'Guys, we're giving away the series' fifth season ending.'"

Even Echevarria, who no longer was involved, had second thoughts. "After the 'Pilot' was successful, I called Scott and Ira and asked if there still was time to edit out the reveal," he says. "But it was too late."

"So we gave away the farm," Behr admits. "I like there being mystery. I like there being things that the audience isn't sure of. And," Behr sighs, "if we hadn't done it, this would have been a very different series."

Although the writers were required to reveal *who* had abducted the 4400, they were careful not to reveal the *why*. "We had a big to-do about how much the future

White Light

Above: Danny Farrell (Kaj-Erik Eriksen) narrowly survives a deadly "life-suck" from brother Shawn.

would tell Tom," Behr comments.

"We made about ten passes at writing the scene on the beach," Craig Sweeny confirms. "When 'Future Kyle' speaks, we went through a very slow and painstaking series of iterations — 'That's too much, that's too little, that's too much' — until we thought it worked."

Armed with the completed script, the cast and crew spent two long nights on the shore of Bunsen Lake shooting the revelation scene. "I was excited," Chad Faust says. "Up to this point I had only worked with Patrick and Joel. Now I had scenes with Jacqui and Peter Coyote and Mark Valley, who played Lytell."

After they had completed most of the sequence, the time came to shoot Tom and Kyle facing one another, frozen in the beam of the 10,000 watt lamp mounted overhead. "It was about six o'clock in the morning," Faust says, "so the sun was

NTAC INFORMATION ARCHIVE

"In 'White Light', Jordan makes a grab for Lily and gets zapped by the baby," Laura Allen says, describing a day on the set. "That's what gives Richard and Lily a chance to drive away. Well, shooting the scene, I threw Billy Campbell away from me and Ali and I went to the car. I got in on the passenger side and Ali, as Richard, got in the driver's seat. He was supposed to start the car and drive off," Allen chuckles. "But instead, we just sat there until Ali turned to me and said, 'Lily, do you have the keys?' The camera was rolling — but someone had forgotten to give him the keys. It was one of the funniest moments."

about to come up and we had to get that shot."

And that's when the trouble started.

"I had anticipated a problem," Joel Gretsch says, "because Chad and I just crack each other up, especially if something is awkward. We had to stare at each other, which is really hard — especially with other people doing dialogue behind us. So in the midst of my concern about it, I said, 'This is what I'm going to do,' and I grabbed Chad by both shoulders. Well, he burst out laughing — and couldn't stop. Then I started and we were both gone."

"We just couldn't contain our laughter," Faust says. "Scott Peters came up to us a couple of times and told us to straighten up. But that didn't help."

"We were like two little boys in church," Gretsch chuckles.

"And then Peter Coyote came over and looked at me and said, 'Just so you know, kid, eighty people are waiting on you right now,'" adds Faust. "That's when the weight of the situation sunk in, and I felt terrible." As dawn broke over the site, the group finished the scene.

"Afterward, Peter said to me, 'You know I was just screwing with you because we had to get the shot,'" Faust notes. "He's a real veteran."

Having resolved Tom Baldwin's situation with his son, the scene originally was meant to end the episode — until Ira Behr thought better of it. "I told the network that if we ended with the father and son on the beach, the series was over," he says. "We'd be telling the audience, 'Good night. Go home. Drive safely.' And we didn't want to say that. We needed a stinger ending with a cool move that would make them want to come back."

As Behr, Sweeny and Robert Wolfe discussed that idea, they thought about Lily and Richard, who they'd sent unceremoniously fleeing from Jordan Collier's housing development — along with the fact that they'd made Lily pregnant. "We needed an antagonist," Behr says, "and the baby was the joker in the pack. She hadn't been taken — but she'd come back, so she wasn't part of the future's plan."

The image of a woman inexplicably with child traveling with a man who is not the father reminded the writers of a more familiar couple, Mary and Joseph on the road to Nazareth. "It's fair to say that some of the imagery was intentional," Wolfe comments. "We wanted to call on those archetypal cultural images because audiences understand them right away, and you can do some interesting storytelling with them."

But the Western world's most studied nativity, which drew a guiding star in the East, wasn't the group's only inspiration. "Robert came up with the idea of the trees bending. That was fantastic," Behr enthuses. "Lily's about to give birth, and the trees are bending to the baby. And that baby's really powerful. In my mind, she was like the Star Child at the end of *2001*." ○

"No one said stopping the future was going to be easy." — Diana Skouris

The miniseries had performed beyond everyone's expectations, and the producers had begun referring to those six hours as "the first season". Yet by November of 2004, the hoped-for call from the network regarding *The 4400*'s second season still hadn't come. "Waiting was brutal," Maira Suro says. "We'd ended on a really high note, and we were wondering, 'What is there to think about? We're huge!'"

"We'd always intended to pick it up," USA Network's Jeff Wachtel says. "But a lot was shaking up around us." That's putting it mildly. USA's corporate overseer, Universal, had just been acquired by NBC, while across town, Viacom Productions was being dissolved and its shows folded into Paramount. "Suddenly all the negotiations were between bigger entities," Wachtel notes. "So it took a while."

In the meantime, the affected personnel were hardly idle. Ira Steven Behr accepted the position of consulting producer and writer on *Dr. Vegas*. Peter Coyote took recurring roles on *The Inside* and *Commander in Chief*. Billy Campbell finalized plans for a year-long voyage around the world on a tall ship. And the entire Canadian crew moved on to other shows. As for the sets — "The owners demolished their building," Perry Simon sighs. "We didn't have a choice; we had to move out."

But despite what felt like an interminable delay, the principal actors really hoped the show would resume. "Before we started season two, I had a lot of time to think about whether to continue," Joel Gretsch comments. "My wife and I had just had a baby. I'd been away from home shooting up in Vancouver for almost four months before my child was born, so I was concerned about going back up. Then I was offered a role in something else that was shooting in Los Angeles. So it was a really tough decision for me to make. But there was just no doubt what I wanted to do, because I love the cast and the crew and the producers of *The 4400*. For me, continuing on the show was, in part, a compliment to them."

Finally the call came, although rather unceremoniously. "The show got picked up and it was just, 'Okay, guys,'" Ira Behr laughs. By this time, *Dr. Vegas* had completed its limited run, leaving Behr free to let his thoughts return to the returnees. "So Craig Sweeny and I started to have lunch meetings at Jerry's Deli in the San Fernando Valley."

"We had nothing written, because it would have been foolhardy to be writing with no real season ahead," says Sweeny. "We'd talk about where we might go with the characters, and then we'd play pin-ball."

"We started at square one, redefining everything," Behr confirms. "We asked

ourselves, 'What is this show? What do we *want* it to be? Who are these people?'"

"We began actual writing just before Christmas," Sweeny says, "for an episode that would go into production in February."

USA's order was for a total of thirteen hours. Although broadcast television typically schedules twenty-two episodes per season, basic cable's scheduling reflects more specialized needs. "We've defined ourselves as a summer series, so thirteen episodes is really the perfect number," Perry Simon explains. "We live in that world and make it work."

With an assignment for a two-hour opener and eleven one-hour scripts, Behr again faced the task of filling out his writing staff. Robert Hewitt Wolfe was already in pre-production on a different show and unavailable, which is why only Behr and Sweeny met at the deli. "I basically had nothing else going," Sweeny says, "so I was happy to hang around. And it was great, because I was becoming a professional for the first time in my life."

"Craig got a real education in a real hurry," Behr concurs.

The first new face invited to join the writing team was Lisa Melamed, whose credits included *Sisters*, *Mad About You*, and *Charles in Charge*. Next came Frederick Rappaport, who'd served with Behr on *The Twilight Zone* and written for *Star Trek: Deep Space Nine*.

"Ira came up with a formula that was tough to adhere to," Rappaport says. "He wanted each episode to have four or five different storylines going at once. The most I'd ever done in a show before was three."

Above: Meet the new boss. Nina Jarvis (Samantha Ferris) brings a new dynamic to the NTAC offices.

Getting such a belated green light "put us behind," Rappaport continues. "We were fighting the rolling production monster for the entire season. It's best if you can stay five scripts ahead of filming, or even three. But we got down to being only one show ahead." For Behr and Sweeny, it was reminiscent of the period a year earlier when the whole writing staff jointly worked on numerous scripts each day. As Rappaport says, "We were just gangbanging scripts."

"Fans of the show would be surprised to know how much of the story emerges just from which actors we have and which ones we don't have that week," Sweeny offers. "Because Peter Coyote was working elsewhere, we created Nina Jarvis as his character's replacement. When we learned that Billy Campbell was going to be away for a year, we decided to kill his character, Jordan Collier."

"The show is a living, breathing thing," Behr explains, "and the story is going to take you where it wants to take you."

Sometimes it can even take you right back where you'd intended to go in the first place. "Originally I had envisioned Shawn emerging as the leader of the 4400," notes Scott Peters. "And he gets there, after Jordan is killed."

A more concrete — or rather, brick and mortar — situation also affected the storyline. As season one ended, Collier was trying to gather the returnees in his large neighborhood housing development. But as season two opens, the housing development is gone, and Collier's plans have evolved into creating the 4400 Center. Having a film crew regularly working nearby can be very disruptive to the lives of real families. "We just couldn't continually shoot in a neighborhood like that," Billy Campbell explains. "So the writers had Jordan create the 4400 Center, which I think is so much... ickier... than a simple neighborhood."

When it came time to replace Coyote's character, word went out for someone who could be just as tough as Ryland. Enter Samantha Ferris to play new character Nina Jarvis. "Lisa Melamed had worked with Samantha on a show called *The Ranch*, and recommended her," Behr says. "She's a really good actress, and fulfills that role completely. Whatever we've given her to do, Samantha pulls it off."

"I'm thrilled to work with her," Jacqueline McKenzie says. "Samantha's really funny, nothing like her character — just a fantastically vibrant, rockin' chick."

Billy Campbell's replacement would be needed just prior to the season's midpoint, but the writers began thinking about it as soon as they heard the details of his tall ship voyage. Although the network would have liked for them to hunt up a Campbell clone, the producers opted for a very different direction by casting Garrett Dillahunt, who had impressed them as he played two very different characters on HBO's *Deadwood*.

As the episodes were written, a number of other casting choices would have to be made for new ongoing characters, including Kavan Smith as NTAC Agent Garrity, Natasha Gregson Wagner as Diana Skouris's sister April, and Jeffrey Combs as "the father of the 4400", Dr Kevin Burkhoff. And a baby would appear in the first episode — character name: Isabelle.

Meanwhile, following the dissolution of Viacom Productions, Perry Simon joined the show as executive producer, and he, Suro and Peters took on production concerns in Vancouver. With the remnants of the *Jake 2.0* sets a thing of the past, the production moved into two soundstages at Lion's Gate Studios, a professional location that had housed such shows as *Dark Angel* and *Battlestar Galactica*. The move made Conchita Campbell very happy. "I had worked at Lion's Gate before, so I knew it better," the young actress says. "Being there was comfortable, and a bit easier."

Everyone in the cast and crew appreciated the opportunities that a longer season would provide, chief among them the breadth it would add to the story possibilities. "During the first season we had so much story to tell and so little time to tell it that we still had permutations of the storylines running around in our heads," Scott Peters says. But a brand new storyline was one of the first priorities. "The network insists on opening with two-hour episodes," Behr says. "Well, those are tough, but we wanted something mysterious to come out of the last moment of that opening two hours. The prediction that 'Mommy's bosses will be punished,' struck us as a really cool thing."

That line of dialogue was the first step in a seasonal master plan — "Sort of," Behr hedges. "Craig and I wanted to answer the questions as to why some returnees had abilities and some did not," the showrunner notes. "Why didn't they just send everyone back with abilities? Why were some people getting abilities six months later? We felt that we needed to plug that hole a little bit. The idea that someone has been messing with them seemed like a good way to go."

With that "someone" being NTAC, and the means of "messing with them" being a drug called promicin, "it's one of the best things we did," Behr says. "The season had some growing pains, and some of the episodes following that opening two hours were a little weak," he admits. "But from that idea, we developed the two-parter 'The Fifth Page' and 'Mommy's Bosses', so we were able to end season two with such a bang that the network, the studio, the producers, the writing staff, and the audience all seemed to be completely on the same page. It was a nice way to go out." ○

Above: Not exactly a traditional family. The Skouris women spend a quiet evening viewing April's (Natasha Gregson-Wagner) tattoo designs.

Wake-Up Call

Written by: Ira Steven Behr & Craig Sweeny
Directed by: Leslie Libman

Guest Cast: Billy Campbell (Jordan Collier), Richard Kahan (Marco Pacella), Charles Napier (Josiah), Summer Glau (Tess Doerner), Jeffrey Combs (Kevin Burkhoff), Rob LaBelle (Dr Nicholas Clayton), Kavan Smith (Garrity)

A year has passed since Tom Baldwin learned the 4400 were taken by future humans in order to prevent a catastrophe that will destroy humanity. The Seattle Home Sec office is now known as the Pacific Northwest division for National Threat Assessment Command (NTAC). Dennis Ryland has been transferred to Washington D.C., replaced by Director Nina Jarvis, who is much more by the book than Ryland. She's kept Tom assigned to desk duty for months, penance for drawing a gun on Agent Lytell.

Tom's son Kyle has been living under observation at NTAC, forced to endure tests that reveal no new information. Tom's former partner, Diana Skouris, lobbies for his return to field duty, but Tom has one caveat before he accepts reinstatement: let Kyle come home. Jarvis agrees to both requests, but tells Tom that if she has any reason to doubt him, he's out.

New families have formed in the past year. Diana has adopted Maia as her daughter, while Richard and Lily Tyler are the parents of six-month-old baby Isabelle. They live inconspicuously in a small town, hoping to avoid the attention of NTAC and Jordan Collier.

Collier, too, has put together a family. He's opened the 4400 Center, a research/residential community for returnees and well-heeled members of the public who want to "unlock the 4400 within themselves". Shawn Farrell, estranged from his own family, has become Collier's protégé, using his healing ability to cure those who contribute to the center.

NTAC is contacted by the Abendson Psychiatric Hospital, where returnee Tess Doerner, a diagnosed paranoid schizophrenic, seems to be using her ability to get the inmates and the orderlies to build a bizarre tower. Tess claims that the people from the future put the image of the tower in her head; when it's completed, she says, it will send her back to them. Tess's ability to influence others is powerful. Each day, more people join in to help complete the project, even the director of the hospital and the NTAC agents who accompany Tom and Diana to Abendson. Jarvis feels the project should be treated like an infectious disease — isolated from outsiders and stopped — but Tom feels strongly that it should proceed to its conclusion.

Collier, the self-proclaimed figurehead for the 4400, publishes a book that reveals his "personal insights" into the abduction, including the fact that the returnees were sent home to "save the world". The revelation stirs up new paranoia about the 4400, particularly in small towns like the one in which the Tylers live. When religious zealot Josiah sees Lily with the book, he launches a tirade of invectives against her and Isabelle. Suddenly, powerful winds buffet Josiah, convincing him that Isabelle is the devil's spawn. Lily and Richard hastily leave

town, but it's too late; Josiah and his two sons are closing in, determined to rid Earth of the "abomination".

At Abendson, Diana has been "infected" by the desire to work on the nearly completed tower. When Jarvis arrives with NTAC reinforcements, Tom stalls them long enough for Diana to throw the switch on the tower. Tess waits to be transported, but instead a huge pulse of energy knocks everyone down. Beyond that, nothing seems to happen.

Josiah and his sons, shotguns leveled, apprehend the fleeing returnees, but in seconds, all three are dead: one son the victim of an involuntary blast from Josiah's gun, another of a self-inflicted wound, and Josiah himself of a massive coronary. They were no match for Isabelle.

At the hospital, Tess wonders what went wrong, but Tom and Diana realize that the machine fulfilled its real purpose. It cured Tess's best friend, fellow inmate Kevin Burkhoff. Once a brilliant neuroscientist, Burkhoff was working on awakening dormant neural pathways of the brain when he was stricken with mental illness. Apparently the future people felt that his sidetracked research — which might ultimately awaken 4400-like abilities in normal people — should continue. Now, thanks to Tess's machine, it can.

Above: Diana and Maia celebrate the girl's transition from Rutledge to Skouris.

Above: Kyle pleads with Tom to get NTAC to release him from observation. After all, he's back to normal — isn't he?

At home, Diana discovers that Maia now confines her revelations about the future to a diary. And one of those revelations chills Diana's blood as she reads it, wondering what it means: "Mommy's bosses will be punished for betraying us."

"Maybe crazy is catching." - Tess

"'Wake-Up Call' started with an idea about the population of a town building a monument," Ira Behr says. "We didn't know what the monument was for, but we talked about it being like the Watts Towers [a makeshift conical sculpture of metal and mortar located in central Los Angeles], and we asked ourselves, 'Why would these people build the Watts Towers? What's going on?'" At the same time, a second image was floating in Behr's thoughts. "I remembered the big alien cities from H.P. Lovecraft's 'The Shadow Out Of Time' and I thought, 'It would be cool if someone thought that's what the future is.'"

That image soon led to a story about a returnee actually *remembering* where the 4400 had been taken. "Craig Sweeny and I were very excited about that," says Behr. "In 'White Light', the future (in the form of Kyle) spoke to Tom, and in Tom's mind that makes him responsible for all of them because the future hasn't spoken to anyone else. He's at the center of this whole situation with the 4400s, and he wants to help, because if his family has had to suffer this much, it has to be for a reason. So when this woman tells him she remembers the future, Tom's ready to defend her actions with his life,

NTAC INFORMATION ARCHIVE

"There's a scene in 'Wake-Up Call' with Tom and Diana and Marco standing outside in the rain looking at the tower," Richard Kahan says. "While we were shooting, it was raining outside, and Marco was the only one with an umbrella and not roughing it. Everyone else was working in the muck. Well, at one point in the scene, Marco is holding the umbrella just over himself, and Tom gives Marco a dirty look, grabs the umbrella and pulls it over so they're all sharing it. That move wasn't scripted or rehearsed. It was completely Joel Gretsch's idea."

"For a while, Joel was playing it as if he wanted to kill Marco," says Ira Behr. "We finally had to tell him, 'Hey, Marco's not a member of your family. It's okay that at the beginning Tom was the guy who didn't like the people in the theory room, but the audience really likes Marco, so back off a little.' Because there were times in the dailies when it looked like he was gonna punch him out. Joel was having too much fun!"

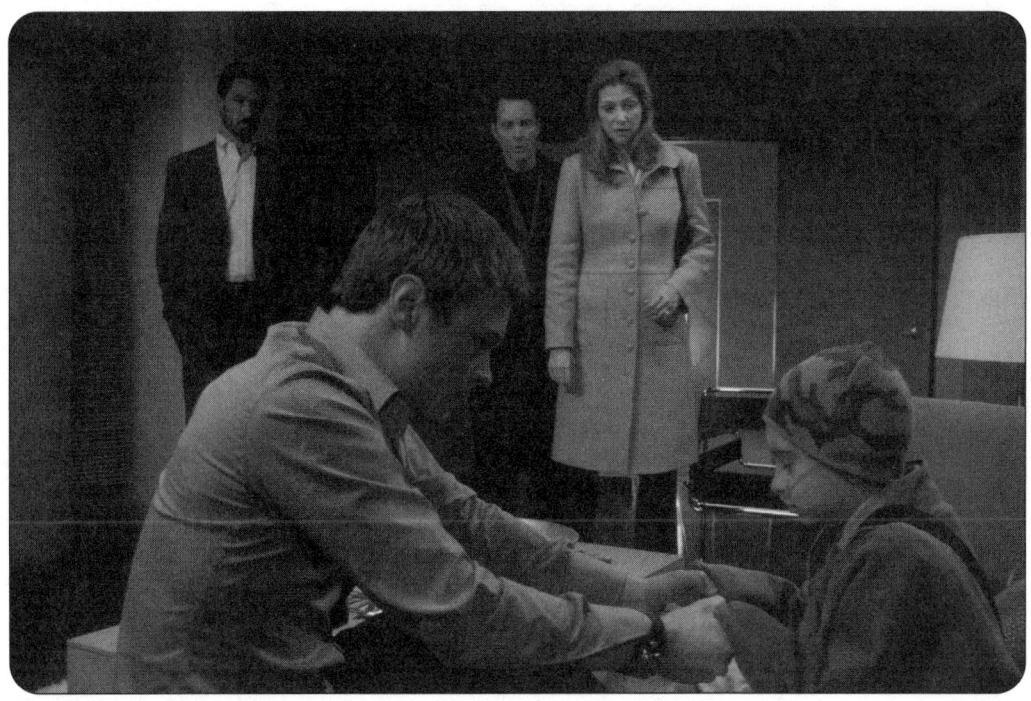

and even go against NTAC.

And that's when Lisa Melamed came up with a great idea. "She said, 'Why don't we do this story in a mental hospital?'" Behr relates. "Suddenly it all came together."

Soon the writers had created mental patient Tess Doerner, who confuses the writings of Lovecraft with memories of being abducted. The producers knew immediately who they wanted to play Tess. Summer Glau had been their first choice to play Lily a year earlier. This time, Glau was available for the show.

As the writers worked to populate the mental hospital, another key character evolved: Kevin Burkhoff. "We'd thought, 'What if there's a guy who's the father of the 4400, a guy that really is what Jordan Collier wants to be?' Well, what actor am I going to think of right off the bat?" Behr asks. "It's a no-brainer."

Behr had been a fan of Jeffrey Combs since seeing him in the 1985 film *Re-Animator* (which was based, coincidentally, on a story by H.P. Lovecraft). His respect for Combs' uncanny ability to portray odd characters grew after he'd hired the actor, first to play various aliens on *Star Trek: Deep Space Nine*, and later on *The Twilight Zone* (2003).

With the right actors in place, serendipity took over. While watching dailies, the producers saw Glau and Combs interacting on screen for the first time, and

Above: Shawn performs a miracle: returning a dying child to health.

Above: Tess Doerner (Summer Glau) designs a device that she believes will return her to the future.

realized they'd stumbled onto a match made in heaven... or at least in purgatory.

"Summer and Jeff are magical together," Behr enthuses. "Even though he's his age and she's her age, you just buy it. When I saw them, I said, 'They're gonna be one of the best relationships on the series.'"

"There was this emotional chemistry, but not sexual chemistry, between Summer and Jeff," Jackie de Crinis says. "It was charming how this young girl was taking care of this older catatonic genius who was a sort of father figure to her."

When he approached Combs, Behr had been honest about the minimal role Kevin played in the initial script. "Ira sort of apologized when he called me for *The 4400*," Combs recalls. "He told me, 'I have a role in a two-parter, but there's not really a lot to it, except that there's a great twist, and the character proves to be pretty pivotal.'" Knowing that Behr had never misled him in the past, Combs agreed to fly to Vancouver.

According to the actor, "Only Ira's brain knows what 'the father of the 4400' means. But to me it meant that I'd probably be back, because the writers were laying the groundwork for future storylines — and they had me in there under the radar."

Combs indeed would return for several appearances later in the season, and Glau would join him in season three as the star-crossed couple, Tess and Kevin, grew in importance.

Meanwhile, other relationships were being developed for the season, including the ones between Shawn and Kyle — and the actors who play them. "Patrick Flueger and I began to hang out together quite a lot," Chad Faust says. "So by this time we were as close as friends can be. Before we shot the scene of Shawn and Kyle walking through downtown in 'Wake-Up Call', we actually rehearsed by walking around Vancouver, going in and out of stores while running our lines. Then we brought that familiarity and comfort to the set."

"Comfort" isn't the word that Laura Allen and Mahershalalhashbaz Ali would use for their experiences during the episode. "'Wake-Up Call' is the episode where Richard and Lily went on the run," Allen says. "I was wearing boots and oversized clothes, and had the baby strapped on as we traipsed up and down those hills. There was something very 'pilgrimage' about it!"

"Being in those woods and working outdoors was fun — when it warmed up!" Ali interjects. "It was February, and we were up in the mountains running along those streams. So it was *freezing*."

"Between shots, the crew set up furnaces for the actors to sit near," Allen says. "Charles Napier, who plays Josiah, has been in dozens of movies, and he started telling us old Hollywood stories, as if we were sitting around a campfire. That was a pleasure. But when he and the fundamentalists started chasing us, Ali and I felt as if we really were being chased, and I actually became afraid of him. Charles was a compelling enemy."

Above: Pursued by a madman, Richard and Lily run for their lives.

Director Leslie Libman shot all of the exterior scenes first, wisely holding the interiors until last in case they should be needed for "rain cover". The interior locations consisted of a cabin and a car. "That cabin was really wonderful, but it was even cold in there," Allen says. "So we were so glad when we finally got that

NTAC INFORMATION ARCHIVE

"Jeffrey Combs is an inventive joy to work with," Jacqueline McKenzie says. "The perfect Jeff moment was after Kevin woke up [in 'Wake-Up Call']. He had an undercurrent of being fixated with Tess Doerner, and even though she's sick, that did not stop. When Kevin went in to say goodbye at the end of the episode, he came up behind her and put a book down. Well, that's when Jeffery did something that wasn't scripted. With his hand, he just swept her hair back from her shoulder. It was the most touching, beautiful grace note," McKenzie says. "When I saw that, I knew that it was true to the fact that Kevin loves Tess. And that's a typical thing for Jeffrey to see and to do.

"I was so happy when I watched that, because for all of us, *The 4400* is an ensemble piece and the show is the star. Anything that makes the show as brilliant as it should be, that reaches the potential that it has on the page, makes you think how very lucky we are we've gotten great guest stars to help with that."

Above: As fundamentalist Josiah, actor Charles Napier was convincing enough to frighten his fellow actors.

old car. What a relief! And also, the baby had a car seat rather than having to hang on my shoulder!"

In the previous season, viewers had become aware of the powerful offspring that Lily was expecting, but now they saw baby Isabelle for the first time. Because of child labor regulations which prohibit long working hours, producers normally use a pair of twins to portray a single baby. Unfortunately, in this case that wasn't possible. "We just couldn't find mixed race twins in Vancouver," Maira Suro says. Faced with that dilemma, the producers initially hired two unrelated children of the same age. "Unfortunately, one of the babies was always crying, so finally we took a chance and just went with little Jordan Lasorsa-Simon — and shot the entire season with only one baby!" Suro says in amazement. "I don't know how we managed it."

Happily, the baby proved to be a real pro. "There were great dailies with her," Suro enthuses. "In a pivotal scene in the cabin, Lily says that they've got to leave because Josiah is chasing them. While Ali and Laura were doing their lines, the baby was making these incredible faces, and because we were all thinking of her as Isabelle, who's aware of everything, we were dying with laughter."

"Little Jordan was six months old when we first got her, and she was such a magnetic presence that I would get drawn into her energy," Laura Allen says. "An actor's priority is to get the shot, but a mother's priority is her child, so having her in my arms made it hard to remember to stay on course with the character.

NTAC INFORMATION ARCHIVE

"In my first episode, I got to go to the exterior 'tower' set," Samantha Ferris recalls. "It was fun, except that my hair is horrible in the rain, and all of the hairdressers got upset.

"I have very curly hair, naturally," explains Ferris. "But curly hair is not as professional looking as I think Nina should be, so we straighten it. It takes an hour and a half, but we can keep it that way for four or five days, with a little bit of work."

"Sam's got ringlets that they straighten with curling irons every day before she goes on set," Jacqueline McKenzie, adds. "And me? I've got straight hair that they put ringlets in before I go on set."

"Jacqui and I," Ferris laughs, "are huge maintenance."

"I'm embarrassed to tell this," Allen offers with a grin, "but all during 'Wake-Up Call' I was wearing Jordan's baby sling incorrectly! Sometimes she seemed uncomfortable, but I've never been a mother, so I didn't know why. Then one weekend I went to visit my friend who was using a sling for her baby. I said, 'I'm wearing one of these on the show,' and put it on. She saw that it was backwards and just fell over laughing at me," the actress says. "After that I wore it correctly." Which, one suspects, baby Jordan appreciated.

For the scenes when the baby's face would not be seen on camera, Jordan was relieved by a less delicate stand-in. "The prop department made a freaky doll for us," Allen reveals. "It looked like a warped, paled-out Chucky [from *Child's Play*]. And it looked water-logged as if it had been left at the bottom of a pool. I almost felt sick just holding it! Then, as time went on, the fingers started to fall off and the hair started to bald out. That doll was not a cuddly thing!"

Given that Isabelle revealed her innate ability by killing Josiah and the fundamentalists, perhaps the comparison to Chucky is appropriate. "Every now and then you want a little bit of a horror show," Behr notes, "and that was it." ○

Above: After Tess's machine brings about an unanticipated effect, Diana and Tom realize that they can't second-guess the future people's motives.

Voices Carry

Written by: Lisa Melamed
Directed by: Vincent Misiano

Guest Cast: Sharif Atkins (Gary Navarro), Natasha Gregson Wagner (April Skouris), Stephen McHattie (Ian Dravitt), Lexa Doig (Wendy Paulson) and Billy Campbell (Jordan Collier)

Minor league baseball player Gary Navarro, a 4400, always harbored hopes of making the majors. Upon his return, he tries to pick up his career where he left off thirty-odd years ago. But although he's still good on the field, something has changed. Suddenly, he can hear the unspoken thoughts of the players — and everyone else he encounters. The constant noise in his head is driving him mad. In desperation, he turns to NTAC, pleading for help. But the higher ups in the organization have an immediate need for Gary's ability. They want him to infiltrate the 4400 Center and find out why known mercenary and arms dealer Ian Dravitt is visiting Jordan Collier. Tom promises Gary that he'll be sent to NTAC Medical as soon as he completes his assignment.

Elsewhere, Richard and Lily suffer the strain of living on the run. They're terrified that the police will connect them to the deaths of the murderous fanatics that Isabelle dispatched, and their money is running short. A troubled Richard confesses his concern about Isabelle's powerful abilities, then experiences a sharp pain in his chest. But it quickly disappears, leaving him wondering if he's suffering from anxiety… or if the baby struck out at him.

As Diana helps Tom monitor Gary's progress at the Center via his implanted transmitter, she contends with an unexpected visit from her 'black sheep' sister April. April wants to stay with her a while — which might not be a good thing for Maia.

Gary's spying hits a snag when Collier's staff confiscates the meds that help him block some of the voices that bombard his mind. Distraught, he barges in on a meeting between Collier and Dravitt and reveals his telepathic abilities. The paranoid Dravitt is about to have Gary killed when Tom and Diana burst into the room to rescue him. Gary reveals that Dravitt is engineering a coup in a small country overseas. Collier, his mysterious business relationship with Dravitt severed, tells Gary that he'd treat him better than NTAC will — and to take care picking the side he wants to be on. Later, when Tom realizes that his boss has loaned Gary to the government for more spying rather than send him to NTAC Medical as promised, the disillusioned agent can't help wondering if Gary wouldn't be better off with Collier.

> **"We're at war here. Don't pick the losing side." - Jordan**

NTAC INFORMATION ARCHIVE

"When we started the series, we were thinking about what government agency to use," Scott Peters comments. "One of the development people at Zoetrope said, 'How about Homeland Security?' That was very new at the time, and nobody really knew what it meant. Then later we made up a division of Homeland Security that doesn't actually exist, the Threat Assessment something or other. That eventually evolved into National Threat Assessment Command."

"We had a hell of a time with the script to 'Voices Carry'," Ira Behr says. "And it never quite made it to where it should have gotten. The ability to read minds is one of those no-brainer abilities. So if NTAC can't help these people, if all they can do is either kill them or use them, then dealing with the 4400 is going

Above: Returnee Gary Navarro (Sharif Atkins) finds that his ability to hear the thoughts of others is driving him mad.

to be harder than anyone had thought."

Behr did like the ending of the episode, with Gary Navarro being taken away for an unnamed assignment. Initially, however, that ending hadn't been a part of the mix. "Navarro was supposed to die," Fred Rappaport explains. "But it seemed more poignant for him to be betrayed and used by NTAC, which is another kind of death."

"'Voices Carry' is one of several episodes in season two in which returnees were going to meet an untimely end, and then, at the last minute, for whatever reason, we said, 'Let's not kill this 4400.' It wasn't necessarily that we were going to bring them back," Behr relates, "it's just that we don't *always* have to bury our guest stars."

In this case, the character received a reprieve for multiple reasons. "Sharif Atkins was one of our big finds," Behr says. "He had the strength and the vulnerability, and I just thought that he was a really good actor."

"And we knew we could use Gary Navarro down the line," Rappaport adds.

"It's always a pleasant surprise when people like Sharif are brought back," Joel Gretsch says. "Jacqui and I will celebrate — 'Oh, we get to work with Sharif, or Summer, or...' Because it's always fun to work with great actors."

Although Navarro survived the episode, his presumed fate — being forced to work for the CIA — was crafted to set up a chain of events that didn't make it into the show. "Tom promised the guy that after this one job they were going to help

Above: Maia and her Aunt April bond immediately.

him — and the fact that he had to break his word was going to send Tom into a very dark place," Behr relates. "He was going to turn to the bottle over his sense of failure. And he was going to stay locked in the bottle throughout most of the second season. We keep trying to mess Tom up," the showrunner says with a chuckle. "It just hasn't happened... yet."

Diana manages to get through the situation with her conscience relatively clean. "Just remember, *I* didn't make that promise to Gary," Jacqueline McKenzie emphasizes. "Diana would *never* promise, because it's not a personal thing with her. Tom invested himself personally, so he gave his word. I didn't give my word.'"

The actions of Nina Jarvis were motivated by a more complicated mindset, Samantha Ferris explains. "In Nina's position you have to turn a blind eye to certain things and do what's best for your job in order to protect yourself, your organization, your people. Nina takes this all very seriously — and that's why she sold Gary Navarro out. I'm sure that she knew the government's plan the whole time, but she couldn't tell Tom and Diana. She may have lost some sleep over it, but that's the job she's chosen to do."

If Diana consciously chose to keep her emotions out of the Navarro case, she couldn't do the same when a surprise visitor showed up at her front door: younger sister April. "I was flattered when they cast Natasha Gregson Wagner as my sister, because she's really beautiful," McKenzie says. "And it's interesting casting, because our personalities are so different from our characters'. Natasha thinks that in reality she's more like Diana, and sometimes I think that I'm more like April, who's arrived to go to a tattoo festival," McKenzie comments. "I'm sure the writers have a really

NTAC INFORMATION ARCHIVE

"One of USA's abilities is to create programming blocks," Jeff Wachtel says. "We paired *The 4400* to *The Dead Zone*, and it was a huge boon, not only to *Dead Zone*, but to our Sunday night, which for the past two summers has ranked number one on cable. Of course, it would have been tough for us to have done that if it hadn't been a science fiction series. Since we already had rolled the dice in that genre once, it made sense to find a compatible, science fiction companion show."

"When Maira, Scott and René first approached us, there was discussion that maybe our sister network, SciFi, would produce and broadcast *The 4400*," Jackie de Crinis adds. "At the time, our brand, Characters Welcome, had not been delineated yet. The irony is that if they had been pitched it a year later, I think *The 4400* would be a SciFi series today. Luckily for us, it got grandfathered in."

good chuckle when they come up with these things!"

"April is very alive and curious and open," Wagner states. "She's much braver than I am. But I think she's very deep, and I really like playing her." When the character first arrives at Diana's home, "she had no idea how meeting Maia was going to affect her. I think April feels that her relationship with Maia is safe, and exists independently of the ups and downs that go on between April and Diana."

Two additional storylines continued to play out during the episode. Richard and Lily were still on the road, where Lily uncharacteristically steals money from a store owner. "The guy behind the counter was such a jerk," Laura Allen says, defending her character. "But we were on the run, and it's what we needed."

"It was desperation," Ira Behr interjects. "They have a baby."

"Up until that point it had been a challenge for me to pull out nuanced performances," Laura Allen comments. "And in that scene, there were so many things going on. The cash drawer is open and I realize that Isabelle is helping me, I'm conflicted by stealing but I really need the money, there's the jerk being mean to me and we've nowhere to live... So I really loved the way Vincent Misiano, the director, handled it. The only dialogue is at the beginning, so during the silent period he actually talked me through it. Now it's one of my favorite scenes."

The remaining storyline — in fact, the raison d'état for NTAC's use of Gary Navarro — involved Jordan Collier and his 'Mob' connection. "We wanted to suggest some real menace, with Collier aligned with the dark side," Behr explains. "The idea of taking over a country as a place for the 4400 to live seemed like a good idea, but none of that got where we wanted it. The whole thing didn't work." ○

Above: Frightened and desperate, Lily steals money — with a little help from baby Isabelle (Jordan Lasorsa-Simon).

Weight Of the World

Written by: Scott Peters
Directed by: Oz Scott

Guest Cast: Natasha Gregson Wagner (April Skouris), Robert Picardo (Trent Appelbaum), Noa Tishby (Chloe Granger), Richard Kahan (Marco Pacella), Lexa Doig (Wendy Paulson), Rhonda Dent (Elise Appelbaum), Michael Rogers (Dimitri Kazar), Jody Thompson (Devon) and Billy Campbell (Jordan Collier)

Returnee Trent Appelbaum feels like a loser. He wants to help out his daughter, who's forced to work at a diner instead of attending college. But he's a washout as a telemarketer, and his loan shark Dimitri wants his money. Trent doesn't have it, so Dimitri guzzles Trent's beer and gives him forty-eight hours to make good. But the next time Trent sees Dimitri, something amazing has happened: he's lost twenty-seven pounds! Dimitri believes Trent's 4400 experience has made him "the Human Diet", and he's willing to forgive the loan if Trent will sip from a bottle of water that he can give to his wife.

Suddenly, major companies are offering Trent top dollar to market his saliva as a revolutionary weight loss product. Trent happily takes high bidder Drandix up on a generous offer.

Meanwhile, celebrity Chloe Granger comes to study at the 4400 Center. Collier welcomes the visit; it means great publicity for the Center. However, Jordan's devoted assistant Devon is dismayed by the attention her boss showers on "his pet superstar", and when she learns that the man she idolizes is sleeping with Chloe, she tries to kill herself. At the hospital, she confesses to Shawn that she can't bear Jordan sharing his special love with someone as unworthy as Chloe.

At the Baldwin household, Tom is furious when Kyle is busted for smashing a store window after overindulging at a frat party. Kyle avoids telling his dad that he has no idea how the incident happened. He's started experiencing strange blackouts and worries that he's relapsing into his post-coma state, when his body wasn't his own.

After Dimitri and his wife die of malnutrition, Trent's world collapses. A protein in his salvia hyper-accelerates human metabolism, making victims burn calories faster than they can accumulate them. His new miracle product is a death sentence, and Drandix already has dosed a hundred test subjects. Worse, Trent's beloved daughter is dying because she drank from his water glass.

The folks in the theory room hypothesize that a restorative serum can be produced from tissue in Trent's liver. After harvesting the organ and replacing it with a donated liver, all 101 lives are saved, and Trent, no longer wealthy, counts his blessings that his daughter is still in this world.

NTAC INFORMATION ARCHIVE

"I asked Jeff Wachtel at some point, 'Which would you rather have, god-like future humans who have such control over what happens in their past that every move they make is some part of a master plan? Or should they be superior human beings that make mistakes, and can't see everything that's gonna happen once they put these people back?'" Ira Behr says. "Well, Jeff already knew the answer that I wanted, and he said, 'Obviously, the latter.' So now the butterfly effect affects everything. They may have meant to take Kyle, but they got Shawn instead. We don't know what guy was sitting at the controls in future central that day, but something went awry."

> **"I worship Jordan." - Devon**

"I found the script to 'Weight of the World' *fascinating*," Jacqueline McKenzie says. "But I couldn't get past the fact that you basically had to tongue kiss Appelbaum to get the effect of his

ability. The passing of saliva is the way you get a lot of diseases, and I really wouldn't want somebody's backwash in a cup!"

That's one reaction to the script. Laura Allen has another. "It's one of my favorite scripts. There are many biblical references in *The 4400*, and 'Weight of the World' was about Greed. This was the first time a 4400 wanted to get rich and famous with his ability, which I think is so true to man's nature. I just loved it."

As diametrically opposed as those two opinions seem, both figured into the concept behind the script. The writers had started with a returnee exploiting his abduction. Saliva is the glue, so to speak, that made the story come together. "Scott Peters had written a draft with the unwieldy title, 'Sold to the Man From NTAC'." Fred Rappaport explains. "It was about a 4400 who had no ability, but was marketing himself as if he did. It was a clever idea, but the story had no heat."

"The guy pretended to be empathic, but he was a phony, and ultimately, we couldn't make it work," Ira Behr says. "But we liked the idea of privatization of the 4400s, and that corporations would want to start buying up people's abilities."

"Craig Sweeny came up with a way to fix it just as we were running out of time," Rappaport continues. "He was stretched out on the couch, all six-foot-three of him, with his feet up, and he started talking about his dog and something about spit. Ira wasn't even in the room; it was just Craig rhapsodizing on spit — and it saved the day."

"When you need a script in a hurry," Behr shrugs, "you end up with spit that enables you to lose weight."

In the episode, Appelbaum isn't the only one trying to exploit the abilities of the 4400. Viewers begin to see that Jordan Collier seems to be taking advantage of his returnee status in any way he can. In a move to recruit the fame and money that the entertainment business can bring to the Center, he pays special attention to Madonna-like celebrity Chloe Granger — much to Shawn's dismay, and to the dismay of Collier's secretary, Devon, played by Jody Thompson. And it was Thompson's performance in particular that sold that part of the plot.

Below: Secretary Devon (Jody Thompson) and Shawn have separate reasons to question the value of the attention Chloe Granger (Noa Tishby) receives when she visits the 4400 Center.

"We had cast Jody to play this little role in the second season opener before we knew the secretary was going to have an affair with Jordan," Behr explains. "But Jody gave the character this true believer quality, like a cult member who's buying the whole cult thing — hook, line and sinker. She was just great." The appreciative producers expanded her role for this episode, and it paid off, Behr says, "We were sorry to see her go, but after Devon's suicide attempt, we didn't know how to bring her back. So we didn't... until the third season."

Is Collier's behavior here — sleeping with one of the Center's

NTAC INFORMATION ARCHIVE

"When René Echevarria first told me about this show, I immediately asked him, 'Do we really need to have the agents and Homeland Security?'" Ira Behr reveals. "Because I saw an *X-Files* comparison coming, and I wondered why, if it was about life interrupted, we would need a police presence all the time. But it was too late, and all of that was a done deal.

"And then, at the beginning, we *did* get all the *X-Files* comparisons, which I don't think was fair. Our agents were never designed to be the solid pole that all the craziness revolves around, like Mary Tyler Moore or Jerry Seinfeld. Tom and Diana are in over their heads the whole time, and are forced to act and react in ways they aren't used to. They were much more complicated than that from right up front."

'students' — out of character for him? Not if you consider character to be a constantly evolving process. "There's a feedback loop that starts," Billy Campbell notes. "You start to play the character, and then the writers start seeing things in you that they like or don't like, so they write toward or away from those things. Then you start to emphasize what they're writing for you, and it just kind of happens. But I can't tell you that anything I did with my secretaries inspired the activity," Campbell jokes.

Above: Be careful what you ask for. Loan Shark Dimitri (Michael Rogers) insists that Trent give some of his weight-reducing saliva to his wife (Katey Wright).

Although this is only the second episode in which viewers see Collier and Shawn in the new 4400 Center, the producers already were well aware as to how they wanted to portray the enterprise. "That's one of the things I came up with," Behr says proudly. "I said, 'We're doing it as a religion!' I was very excited about that. By this time, people had started calling Jordan Collier 'J.C.', and I thought that we may as well follow through on the symbolism." While doing research on cults and pseudo-religions, the staff devised the Keys, the symbols of advancement that viewers first hear about when Collier awards "First Key" status to Chloe. "We shot some really cool scenes showing the ways the Center's staff studied and tested the members," Behr reveals. "They were great scenes to write, but the way they were shot just didn't work and we had to cut them from the show."

Throughout the episode, one plot thread follows Kyle Baldwin as he goes through some initially humdrum days. At first it seems that the character doesn't have much connection to the rest of the show's edgy themes. But things heat up when Kyle apparently blacks out while at a party, only to find himself standing in front of a broken store window just as the police arrive to arrest him. The mystery of Kyle's blackout deepens in the final act, when the character stands before a mirror watching his image fluctuate, vibrate and decompose. The image in the mirror was a composite of two shots. "They filmed me just standing there responding as if I was looking at the being that was inside of me. So that was an interesting thing to try to imagine," Chad Faust says. "And then we went outside to a greenscreen and shot two minutes of me doing some kind of alternative tribal dance with all these body distortions and wild faces. It was the craziest thing you ever saw." ○

Suffer the Children

Written by: Frederick Rappaport
Directed by: Vincent Misiano

Guest Cast: Billy Campbell (Jordan Collier), Kaj-Erik Eriksen (Danny Farrell), Lindy Booth (Liv), Kathryn Gordon (Heather Tobey), Andrew Airlie (Brian Moore), Reece Thompson (Greg Venner)

Teacher Heather Tobey has developed the ability to bring out virtuoso-level artistic talent in certain students. Although many parents are grateful, a vocal minority are frightened of Heather's gift and they file charges of child abuse. Tom and Diana are sent to the town of Fairview to investigate.

At the Center, Collier experiences one of the crippling attacks that he's suffered ever since his brief contact with Lily's unborn child. Shawn is surprised when Collier describes that contact as a gift; the baby "judged him" and found him wanting. But since the encounter, Collier insists, he's devoted his life to a purer purpose.

Far from the Center, Richard and Lily continue to run from both Collier and NTAC, but eventually their luck runs out. Richard is picked up by the police, who report his presence to Collier.

In Fairview, Tom and Diana see the amazing talents Heather has nurtured in the classroom and realize that no crime has been committed. But some of the parents protest Heather's return to the school, particularly the father of Greg Venner. Heather was unable to affect Greg, and although Greg pretends not to care, he's secretly crushed. He sees his father as an embittered failure, and he's frightened that he'll turn out the same way. Desperate, Greg brings a gun to school and demands that Heather change him — or else.

In Seattle, Shawn befriends some homeless teenagers and finds himself attracted to Liv, a tough but pretty girl who seems meant for better things. Collier allows Shawn to help the teens, but warns him never to exhibit his ability in front of them. However, when Liv's boyfriend overdoses, Shawn can't turn away. He saves a life — then finds himself surrounded by a crowd of the lame and the sick, who demand his help.

Shocked by his son's behavior, Greg's father begs the boy to put down the gun. "Just because I failed," he admits, "doesn't mean you have to." Moved, Greg surrenders.

Collier asks Richard to return to Seattle with Lily and the baby, but Richard notes that Jordan pretended to help them before, when all he wanted was the baby. Jordan swears he's changed — and to prove it, he offers to allow Isabelle to judge him again. If she doesn't like what she sees, she'll punish him. Realizing they can't run forever, Richard accepts and introduces Jordan to Isabelle, who — to everyone's surprise — accepts him with a smile.

> **"If you heal one of them, you'll have to heal them all." - Jordan**

"The notion of a kid getting hold of a gun and taking it to school is very potent," Jacqueline McKenzie says. "I don't come from a gun culture, so to me, a child having access to a gun seems

Above: Diana and Tom wonder if bringing out the inherent talents of children can be considered a crime.

specifically American. Of course, that issue isn't what the episode is about. It's about a woman bringing out these amazing abilities in children. The audience should never feel that something is being beaten into their heads in a 'thou shalt' way."

This is not the first time that social commentary found its way into the series, from Dennis Ryland's increasingly rigid interpretation of a certain administration's conservative politics to the prejudice that the 4400 returnees feel on a daily basis. "Social commentary emerges naturally from what the characters are doing," Craig Sweeny says. Or more bluntly, as Fred Rappaport says, "Social commentary? Please. We could never do enough."

Even the fictional parents' reaction to returnee Heather Tobey's impact on her students was social commentary to Ira Behr. "Fundamentally, Heather was going into their children's minds and changing them," he says. "People don't like that. What if tomorrow the kids all suddenly go into lockstep? What if it's just stage one of some strange plan... like, they open up their mouths and little space ships fly out of them?"

But it's through Heather's *inability* to affect young Greg Venner that the most subtle comment is made. "Not all of us are poets," Behr says. "Not all of us are artists. Not all of us have the music of the spheres in us. And that can be a burden."

Suffer the Children

Above: Student Greg Venner (Reece Thompson) insists — at gunpoint — that Heather Tobey (Kathryn Gordon) use her ability to find hidden talents within him.

"When I came onto the show, there was a one-line idea written up on the dry board," Fred Rappaport recalls. It said, 'A teacher who is a muse', which I thought was a great idea and I jumped on it." Rappaport is especially pleased with the bit of color he incorporated into this muse's backstory. "Heather had failed to inspire the students in her classroom before she was taken in 1971, but now she's back and is making a difference," he says. "The father of the boy with the gun had been her student, but you only see a couple of quick moments of that in the episode. Originally, we had a scene where he's threatening her on the phone and she responds by saying, 'You were a bully back then and you're still a bully now.' The kid, Greg, was standing in the corner watching his father make this call, and it helped the kid's arc. We shot it, but we had to cut it because the episode was nine minutes too long.

"We cut another entire subplot of 'Suffer the Children' too," Rappaport reveals. "I'd written a sequence about April using Maia to gamble, and Maia giving her the wrong information. We held it and put it into 'Carrier' three episodes later."

Behr is particularly pleased with the casting in 'Suffer the Children', even if it was an uphill struggle to get the muse in question. "The network wanted us to cast a name, so we tried to get all of these big time actresses," Behr volunteers. "But it was all falling through. Sometimes you get snakebit no matter what you do. You'll wonder, 'What? Is everyone pregnant, just had a baby, on vacation, getting her teeth fixed, having breast surgery?' For whatever reason, we couldn't find anyone, until Craig suggested Kathryn Gordon, who we knew from an episode of *Dr Vegas*. She came in and read, and was really good, but the network

NTAC INFORMATION ARCHIVE

"Little Jordan Lasorsa-Simon was perfect as baby Isabelle," Maira Suro states. "We have hilarious footage of her grabbing Laura's face while she's trying to deliver lines. Everybody loved Jordan. In fact, Ali and Laura wrote her a letter and gave it to Tracy, her mother, so when Jordan gets older she'll have a souvenir from her experiences on the show."

still wanted a name, or even a semi-name. Finally, we hadn't turned up *anyone* else, and time was collapsing, as always, so at the last minute Kathryn got the role. And she did a really sweet and lovely job," Behr concludes. "She was our 'Lana Turner' discovery." And once again, because the actor's work impressed everyone, the character would return in a later season.

Above: If you heal one, they will come. Liv (Lindy Booth) looks on as Shawn inadvertently draws the attention of the homeless community.

Another discovery was Lindy Booth, who appeared as the runaway, Liv. "I saw the runaway story with Shawn as a little darker," notes Rappaport. "And I saw Liv as a little grungier. But then they cast Lindy, who is a model and looked really good with Patrick," Rappaport admits. "When I went up to Vancouver to watch the filming, the crew was calling the character 'The Homeless Hottie'!"

Although Rappaport wrote the final script, he credits Behr with the most striking sequence in Shawn's throughline. "Ira came up with the idea of all these homeless people grabbing at Shawn, making the full impact of his ability as a healer come home to him. He's suddenly overwhelmed by the fact that this motley group is a stand-in for the entire world."

"Doing good is a complicated issue," Behr interjects. "It isn't as easy as it seems, because there's a lot of pain and suffering out there, so where do you draw the line? If you go out into the streets and think you're going to be some holy man who can heal, you'd better watch your ass, because they're gonna come out of the woodwork. That's more than one twenty-year-old guy can handle, no matter how cool his ability."

A subtle edit at the end of that scene, cutting from Shawn's reflection in his car window to Richard's image in a car's side mirror, provides a visual grace note to the episode. Because the scene with Shawn was added to the script so late, it was shot by Scott Peters after director Vincent Misiano had completed work on the rest of the episode. That allowed Peters to match some of Misiano's camera moves. "I remember the scene when Richard gets cornered by the police," Laura Allen says, "because of the way Vincent made use of the glass and the mirrors, both in the car and the mini-mart. Vincent wanted it to be a really powerful moment when Richard is at the door and whispers, 'Go,' to Lily. The way he framed it, it was a very technical shot. We had to stay exactly within our marks, which actually is really wonderful, because without that structure, you can feel really unanchored." ○

As Fate Would Have It

Written by: Craig Sweeny
Directed by: Nick Gomez

Guest Cast: Billy Campbell (Jordan Collier), Natasha Gregson Wagner (April Skouris), Kaj-Erik Eriksen (Danny Farrell), Lindy Booth (Liv), Lexa Doig (Wendy Paulson), Richard Kahan (Marco Pacella), Andrew Airlie (Brian Moore)

After a terrified Maia informs Diana she's had a vision that Jordan Collier will be killed, NTAC scrambles to find the assassin before he or she can fulfill the prophecy. Collier isn't interested in protective custody. He's spent too much time organizing a highly publicized reunion of 4400 members from around the world; he's not about to postpone the event.

Privately, though, Collier is worried. Maia's predictions have never been wrong. When Shawn begs him not to let himself be made a martyr, Collier experiences a rare moment of indecision. He can think of only one person to turn to: Isabelle Tyler. Their first encounter changed his life. Maybe now she can show him what he's meant to do. As Collier quietly entreats the baby to let him in on any insight she may have into his fate, he touches the baby's hand and experiences a rush of images within his mind. He sees himself in the future, receiving adulation from adoring crowds, and a portrait of himself as a much honored, much older man.

Believing that he has his answer, Collier continues plans for the reunion. NTAC, however, remains on alert, and when Tom and Diana apprehend an armed man who's bypassed the Center's security, Collier feels he's literally dodged a bullet.

In the meantime, Lily is overjoyed when Heidi, her daughter with Brian, comes to see her. The little girl has learned the truth about her and wants to become a part of Lily's life. But Lily's happiness is short-lived. After she introduces her to Isabelle, Heidi suffers a ruptured spleen. Brian says the doctors don't understand what happened — but Lily does. Isabelle doesn't want any competition for her mother's love.

Kyle's memory gaps are becoming more prevalent. But although he's frightened, he refuses to discuss the blackouts with his father.

On the day of the reunion, security is tight but fate has the upper hand, and a sniper fulfills Maia's prophecy. As Collier dies, he realizes that Isabelle lied to him...

Later that day, Shawn is shocked to learn that Collier's body has disappeared from its casket.

That night, a man places the pieces of a disassembled rifle into a gym bag and tosses it into a lake. Then Kyle Baldwin turns and disappears into the darkness.

> **"He's gonna die! I saw it!" - Maia**

It could have been a scene in an Agatha Christie mystery.

"Joel Gretsch, Jacqui McKenzie, Richard Kahan and I were sitting in a room," Chad Faust recalls, "when Scott Peters burst in and said, dramatically, 'There's a killer in this room!' Jacqui asked, 'Do you mean a killing in the line of duty?' and Scott said, 'No. Not in the line of duty. It's *murder.*'

"Scott refused to answer any more questions," Faust laughs. "So that became a

running gag on the set — 'There's a killer in this room.' We didn't know who or why until the script to 'As Fate Would Have It' showed up."

And that's when Faust realized that he was the one who'd been fingered.

"We'd had a whole different storyline planned for Kyle," scriptwriter, Craig Sweeny says. "But Billy Campbell was leaving, so we went back and added Kyle's blackout scenes to the previous two scripts. We were hinting, 'Pay attention to this character,' because we wanted the revelation that Kyle was the shooter to come out of left field."

"Kyle had become a very difficult character for us," Ira Behr explains. "We had Chad for all thirteen episodes, but no story for him. He was playing this moribund character that wasn't going anyplace. Sure, we sent Kyle to college and gave him a girl, Wendy, to be interested in, but the scenes we shot were always the first to land on the cutting room floor. While we were talking about Billy Campbell's trip and how we would get rid of Jordan Collier, I said, almost as a joke, 'The one who should kill Collier is *Kyle*, but we can't do that.' There was a long pause," Behr says. "Then Craig said, 'Well, why *can't* we do that?'" And suddenly it went around the writer's room like wildfire — 'Yeah,

Above: Jordan Collier learns too late that Isabelle is as manipulative as he is.

NTAC INFORMATION ARCHIVE

The song Jordan is attempting to sing to Isabelle is 'All the Pretty Little Horses'. "Of course, when we wrote the scene, we didn't know that Billy can't sing," Ira Behr laughs.

Above: Lily finally has a happy reunion with her daughter Heidi (Genevieve Buechner).

that's perfect! He'll be featured the whole second half of the season! There'll be a reason for Kyle Baldwin to be on this show!'"

No one was more surprised than the actor. "I thought that maybe Wendy would turn out to be a spy for Jordan," Faust notes. "Or maybe this was just a moment for Kyle to have a normal life for once. It turned out only to be a little calm before the darkness of the assassination storm."

"A lot of the things in season two exist only because Billy had a boat trip planned," Behr adds. "Even Richard and Lily's throughline changed. They were going to be on the road longer, but with Billy leaving, Shawn would have been the only character at the Center. So we brought them back early."

Campbell's long-planned trip around the world on the sailing ship *Picton Castle* was not his first experience on the high seas. "I've been sailing on tall ships for about five years now," the actor — and sailor — says. The *Picton Castle* is a true working tall ship, with a crew of fifty-two handling the 179-foot, steel-hulled, three-masted barque. Built in 1928, the vessel carries 12,450 square feet of canvas sail. "I told the producers, 'I'm getting on a sailboat and I'm not going to be anywhere you can reach me until the moment the boat touches the place that it left from a year earlier. I'm not just sailing around — I'm sailing around the *planet*.' As it happened, the trip took thirteen months."

The following season — thirteen months later — Campbell again would appear on *The 4400*, but did that trip get the sea out of his system? "I'm now studying to get my Able Seaman's license — and eventually my Captain's license," he says happily.

Jordan Collier's assassination affected all of the show's characters, from Maia, who predicted it, to Isabelle, who lied to guarantee it. The idea for Isabelle to mislead Collier came late in the writing process. "We had a different reason for Jordan's going through with the reunion party," Sweeny comments. "But while I

NTAC INFORMATION ARCHIVE

Behind every cloud is a silver lining. A case in point: "I love TV shows that mix humor into the dramatic pressure," Craig Sweeny offers. "The best one, I think, was *Buffy the Vampire Slayer*. But humor just doesn't work for us. Our show started with Tom's divorce and his son's coma, so the tone happened organically."

"That's what's good about it," Joel Gretsch jokes. "I love the fact that the overall scope of the show mirrors Tom's life. That's just great!"

was working on the script I really got stuck. After about three days of nothing happening, I was so stuck that I went off to play video poker! Sometimes you just can't think about it anymore, you know? And as I was driving back home, I realized that the key to it is that he finally has the baby back there. That's who he had wanted all along, and it was his hubris in having the baby that would lead to his death. Once I had that, I had the whole episode. It led to his going to Isabelle to seek advice, and to her showing him what he wanted to see. It was a breakthrough moment."

The episode closed with two classic images, one reflecting a reverential source and one offering a bit of an homage to a Hollywood classic. Collier's new secretary, Lucy, is stunned to find that Collier's body has disappeared from the interment room, a scene not unlike that of Mary Magdalene discovering the empty tomb of Jesus. "It's hard to avoid that kind of comparison anytime you begin hinting at resurrection," Sweeny says.

Above: Despite his best efforts, a distraught Shawn is unable to save Jordan Collier's life.

And for the final image, ex-addict Liv comes to see Shawn as he assumes responsibilities as the new head of the Center. But before she can speak to him, a bodyguard slowly closes the door, leaving her out in the cold. "It occurred to me that Shawn's coming to power was very much like Michael Corleone coming to power at the end of *The Godfather*," admits Sweeny. "So I thought that it would be fun just to incorporate that image. I mean, Francis Ford Coppola *is* one of the producers of our show, so it's a nice tip of the hat." O

Life Interrupted

Written by: Ira Steven Behr
Directed by: Michael Watkins

Guest Cast: Karina Lombard (Alana Mareva), Kaj-Erik Erikson (Danny Farrell), Brooke Nevin (Nikki Hudson), Chilton Crane (Susan Farrell), Kevan Smith (Garrity)

Tom Baldwin awakens to discover that nearly every aspect of his life has changed. He has a son who *looks* like Kyle, but is well-adjusted and heading for medical school. He has a beautiful wife named Alana who's a complete stranger. He's still an agent for NTAC, partnered with Diana Skouris, but no one has ever heard of the 4400. Their present priority is a terrorist cell, and they're about to take down Dougherty — one of its members — at the 'Collier Museum', site of the 4400 Center in Tom's reality. Tom assists in apprehending Doherty, but while he's at the museum, he spots a black obsidian door. He glimpses only shadows as he peers through a window in the door, but somehow knows that the eerie room is connected to the 4400. A second later, however, it's just an ordinary door, leading to a storage room.

Haunted by his vision and unable to cope with the altered realities of his life, Tom returns to the museum. There's nothing *in* the storage room, but he finds it preferable to the unfamiliar world outside. A troubled Diana has Tom placed under psychiatric care at NTAC. When Tom's wife Alana arrives, he's uninterested in talking to her until she reveals that she, too, is new to this reality. She doesn't recall marrying him, but she *does* recall she's a 4400! And she wants Tom to help her find out what's going on.

Tom convinces the doctors that he's well enough to be released so he and Alana can try to solve their mystery together. But aside from their memories, there are no clues. As the weeks pass, they fall in love. The world they're living in may not feel real, but the connection they've found with each other does.

NTAC INFORMATION ARCHIVE

The final scenes in 'Life Interrupted' take place eight years down the road from now, which obviously kept the hairdressers on *The 4400* busy. Garrity sports a mustache, Shawn a trendy 'soul patch', Diana a short new hairdo, Tom some distinguished gray at the temples and Danny...

"They gave *me* that ridiculous used-car salesman moustache," Kaj Eriksen says. "I had to go in for a moustache fitting! And out of the whole bunch of choices, they picked the goofiest looking one! Everybody gave me a hard time about it, and I felt so cheesy wearing it."

"Yeah," Ira Behr agrees. "They did put that stupid moustache on Kaj."

Years pass, where everyone Tom knows is living a happier life than they had in his reality. Yet when Tom again glimpses the obsidian door, he's unable to resist the temptation to open it.

Inside, he finds Alana — or rather, a program from the future that looks like her. The program explains that the real Alana has the ability to create new realities within her own mind. She and Tom have been living within *this* reality for the past eight years — although only minutes have passed in Tom's old reality. The future people wanted Tom and Alana to fall in love, to give him a source of strength that will sustain him as he faces the terrible trials ahead.

Neither Tom nor the real Alana wish to leave this perfect reality. Yet if they don't, humanity will not survive. Reluctantly, the couple bids farewell to the inhabitants of their utopia — and then Alana wills it out of existence.

Suddenly, Tom finds himself back in his old reality, where all is as he left it, except for one thing. There is a 4400 named Alana Mareva who remembers their life together. When Tom encounters

her outside the NTAC building, the two fall into a loving embrace. Their 'past' may be behind them — but now they have the ability to create a real future.

> **"This is not the same world it was yesterday." - Tom**

"When I read the script to 'As Fate Would Have It', I couldn't believe how brilliant it was," Jacqueline McKenzie enthuses. "And the production came together so beautifully that I asked the producers, 'How are you ever going to follow this?' I mean, it was only halfway through the season, and I actually started to get a little panicked," she admits. "Then they gave us the script for 'Life Interrupted', and I thought, 'Ira Behr is a complete genius.' Rather than try and better it, he took a hairpin turn. My next thought was, 'God, I'm in such good hands.'"

"'Life Interrupted' is either The Best of Ira Behr or The Worst of Ira Behr," observes *The 4400*'s showrunner with a laugh, "because the idea of taking the audience to an emotional high point with Collier's assassination, and then throwing them what clearly is meant to be a curve ball, was risky. The episode is kind of my *Bring Me the Head of Alfredo Garcia*, which is the most 'out there' Sam Peckinpah movie, but the only movie that Peckinpah ever made without any studio

Above: Mr and Mrs Baldwin. Alana Mareva (Karina Lombard) and Tom renew their marriage vows in the altered reality where only they remember the 4400.

interference. He used to tell people, 'If you don't like that one, you really don't like my movies. You may think you do, but that one is pure me.' So 'Life Interrupted' may be out there, but I stand by it," Behr concludes. "And I have to give the USA Network credit, because everyone there stood by it too."

"Ira pitched 'Life Interrupted' to me at the start of the second season, and it was unbelievably imaginative and exciting," says Maira Suro. "But I was concerned that it would be confusing, and people would wonder what was going on. Then we had our meeting with USA."

Before principle photography started on season two, the producers met with the USA executives to pitch the first six hours (the two-hour opener, and four additional episodes) they'd planned — essentially half of the season. "It was a long meeting," Suro says, "about five hours. And then at the very end, Ira said, 'Now let me give you a little taste of what episode seven is going to be.' When he finished talking, they were a little nervous, but they took the leap."

"Of course," Behr admits, "halfway through breaking the story, the whole thing started to fall apart. We had scenes where Tom meets himself in the alternate universe. He was a comic book writer doing a story about 4400 people landing on Earth, and that's how he realizes the truth of where he belongs. But it just got crazy, and I was ready to say, '*No mas, no mas*, I surrender.' After that it was slash and burn. 'Simplify!' became our clarion call."

But when the script finally came in, no one was disappointed. "I still remember

NTAC INFORMATION ARCHIVE

"We really liked the 'future room' that only Tom can see," Ira Behr says. "But you don't really know what will work until you get some response. So Craig kept saying to me, and the studio executives kept saying to me, 'We cannot go to this place too often. We don't want to see the future too much.' And I think that's true. So we didn't see it again until the next season. But for that one moment, I thought the future room was a really cool place."

how hard my heart was beating after I finished reading it," says Suro. "All I could say to Ira was, 'Wow!'"

"I'd called 'Life Interrupted' a 'palate cleanser' when I pitched it to the network," Behr explains. "But here's the bottom line. The episode really isn't a one-off. It really wasn't indulgent. Because what came out of it is very important to the series. It told us all kinds of stuff: that the future is watching Tom Baldwin; that the future needs Tom Baldwin; that Tom Baldwin is a hero. I

Above: She only *looks* like Alana. Tom meets with a representative from the future who warns him of the trials ahead.

mean, a lot of people would have stayed in that fantasy world, because, as Diana says, even if the real world *is* the real world, why go back? But Tom chose to do the brave thing and come back. To me, that's why Tom is the hero. Not because he arrests people, but because he will commit to the action that he has to take and he will follow it through."

"Coming into season two, I'd known *something* was going to happen," Joel Gretsch comments. "The producers told me, 'Episode seven is coming your way. It's going to have some interesting stuff for you.' And when I finally got to read it, my first thought was, 'I have a lot of work to do!'" he laughs. "Tom had to say goodbye to all the people he loved, knowing that he might not see them again. He had to have faith and trust because he didn't know if his plan with Alana was going to work. That's the element in the story that I liked."

"And it gave me an opportunity to go inside my character and answer questions about what makes Tom tick," Gretsch adds. "Now I keep hoping that they do episodes like this featuring each of the characters, so the whole cast can have that opportunity."

"The episode had really mixed reactions from the fans." Craig Sweeny points out. "Some of the people on the web said that this was the end of *The 4400* because we had jerked them out of the series narrative. But over time I think they came to appreciate it."

"'Life Interrupted' is probably USA's favorite episode of the whole series," Behr comments. "Michael Watkins directed the hell out of it. He got great performances out of everybody. Especially Joel," Behr concludes. "He just shines." ○

Carrier

Written by: Douglas Petrie
Directed by: Leslie Libman

Guest Cast: Sherilyn Fenn (Jean DeLynn Baker), Natasha Gregson Wagner (April Skouris), Karina Lombard (Alana Mareva), Richard Kahan (Marco Pacella), Kavan Smith (Garrity) and Garret Dillahunt (Matthew Ross)

Attempts at family bonding are the order of the day in Seattle. At the Baldwin household, Kyle tries to wrap his head around the news that his father met, married and lived with Alana for years — all within the course of a few minutes. Kyle finds Alana's familiarity with him a bit off-putting, and her conviction that he can become anything he wants, despite having spent three years in a coma, even more so. Nevertheless, her warm nature and culinary skills begin to win him over.

At the Skouris household, Maia enjoys the company of April, but wonders if her aunt likes her for herself or for her ability to help her win gambling wagers.

At the 4400 Center, Shawn finds the task of filling Jordan Collier's shoes an overwhelming mandate. Enter Matthew Ross, a lobbyist for the Center. Ross explains that Collier had asked him to assist Shawn if he wasn't around to do it. Shawn appreciates the help but balks at Ross's heavy-handed attempts to guide him.

In the meantime, life in Granite Pass has taken a definite turn for the worse. The entire populace is dead, victims of a fast-acting lethal virus. Only one resident seems to have survived the biological scourge; the body of Jean Baker has not been accounted for. Seeing as Baker is a 4400, NTAC assumes that her ability either protected her from the outbreak... or caused it.

NTAC INFORMATION ARCHIVE

"Joel and I couldn't stop laughing while we were shooting the street scene in 'Carrier,'" Jacqueline McKenzie says. "They made us put on these white contamination suits, and we looked so ridiculous that the first thing we did was start moon-walking. There was no way to breathe in them — and halfway through the first shot I couldn't see Joel because the inside of his mask had fogged over!

"And then," McKenzie says, catching her breath between giggles, "this technician dude comes over to Tom and Diana and just lifts off his helmet. Now, I know that he said it wasn't necessary anymore — that the danger was over — but as a scientist, I think they shouldn't have been so easy to take off. I mean, they should have been sealed and pressurized, but there was no connection between the helmet and the suit.

"Sometimes silly things distract you from doing your job," notes McKenzie, "and that day, it was those suits."

As NTAC begins to look for her, Jean Baker holes up in a motel and places a phone call to the Center, asking for help. Ross reports the call to NTAC, and a team of agents in bio-gear is sent to the motel. But their strong-arm tactics frighten Jean, which causes the sores on her palms to swell and burst open. In seconds, the agents are dead, despite their protective garments. Jean flees from the motel, taking one of the agent's cars. Finding a cell phone inside, she hits a button and finds herself connected to Tom Baldwin. Sobbing, Jean explains that the agents' deaths aren't her fault. Tom quickly realizes who's calling and what has transpired. He offers to help her, but Jean says she knows now that no one can help her. It's up to her to end this catastrophe. And she hangs up.

As Tom and Diana attempt to track Jean down, Marco explains that Jean's body has been turned into a delivery system for the toxic virus she carries within her. Whenever she gets upset, the virus becomes airborne.

Believing that Jean plans to kill herself, Tom and Diana rush to the scene of a burning car — the car Jean stole. But her body isn't inside. She's changed her mind, she reveals in another call to Tom.

She now believes that she was given her ability in order to purify humanity, and she plans to carry out that plan. Racing against time, Tom and Diana track her to a busy square in the middle of Portland. Tom pleads with Jean to reconsider, but she's convinced it's too late. With no other choice, Diana fires her weapon, killing Jean and putting an end to the plague.

A weary Tom returns home to Alana's loving arms. Upstairs, Kyle is feeling optimistic about his future — maybe medical school *isn't* such a crazy idea — until he suddenly remembers everything that happened during his blackouts. *He murdered Jordan Collier!*

"Don't piss her off." - Marco

"When we were tweaking the 'Pilot' to the series, we had a lot of conversations about Orson Bailey's ability and how he used it," Maira Suro comments. "We decided that it really wasn't under his control; it was all being generated by his anxiety. And that's the way it was with Jean DeLynn Baker, the 'pizza hand lady'."

Baker's anxiety caused her to release spores in much the same way that mushrooms and fungi do. The result is uniquely horrifying. "That was to shake things up," Fred Rappaport says. "It's very important to the arc of the series that the public keeps demonizing the 4400, so sometimes we need a legitimate demon. In the first season, only Knox, the serial killer, had been what I call an 'ooga booga' 4400. In the second season, Heather the art teacher certainly wasn't a demon, except to a bunch of small-minded hicks. But Baker is a legitimate threat. You can see her

Above: Last woman standing. Jean DeLynn Baker (Sherilyn Fenn) realizes that she caused the death of every person in her home town.

as a metaphor for AIDS, or any other plague. And that's why we had the truck driver come up with a biblical prophesy to give her. Suddenly she can think of herself as a walking prophesy."

"One of the ultimate statements about the human condition is, to quote Renoir's film *The Rules of the Game*, 'Everyone has his reasons,'" Ira Behr says. "And her reasons too. Baker's life is a disappointment. She's fighting this impulse, but ultimately she has to give in to it, and she becomes convinced that that's what she's back for. To me, that's pretty cool. It's all religion, and scouring the earth."

While Tom, Diana and NTAC are busy chasing down Baker, Shawn is surprised by the arrival of Jordan Collier's chosen successor, Matthew Ross. "Matthew is a tough love guy," Garrett Dillahunt, the actor who plays the lobbyist, says. "He just walks in thinking, 'I'll run the Center now that my friend Jordan's gone. I'll run it the way I think it should be run — and, yes, I'm a bit rigid, but we'll get things done, damn it.' He's greedy, but in his mind he's doing it for Jordan," the actor says.

Throughout 'Carrier', Marco looks for opportunities to get closer to Diana. "One of the great things about Diana is that she's so focused and involved in her work," says Richard Kahan. "Well, Marco can see that, and he can take it as an opportunity to come in with a fresh cup of coffee for her." Near the end of the episode, he ups the ante by supplying her with a fake version of Maia's diary. "That was such a great moment for my character," Kahan says. "Up to this point you know that Marco loves his job, and that he's like a kid in a candy store when it comes to research. But now you see that he cares so much about Diana that he puts his job on the line to help her out. It's just a great step in rounding out Marco and showing who he is deep down inside.

"For me, the challenge of that diary scene was playing his anticipation of what her reaction would be," Kahan continues. "He knows that he's really putting himself out there revealing what he's feeling for her. But when Diana is so taken aback and appreciative, it seemed natural for Marco to shy away and not fully take credit for what he did.

"When we were shooting that scene, there was a very clear reaction of 'Awwwwwww,' from the females on the set," Kahan laughs. "It was really fun to play. It's one of my favorite scenes."

Another thread running though 'Carrier' concerns Kyle getting to know his dad's girlfriend, Alana. Although Tom and Alana have eight years of memory together, it's all new to Kyle, and he has a bit of trouble adjusting. "The cast had established such a tight community, that when Karina joined us, what was happening between

"Ira came in to the writer's room one day and asked us, 'Do you have any ideas that begin with a town full of dead people?'" Craig Sweeny recalls. Although the staff didn't know it, it was a question that had been on Behr's mind for ten long years.

"In 1995, we did an episode on *Deep Space Nine* where there was a massacre in a sort of internment camp," Ira Behr explains. "Well, I had written that the place was full of dead bodies. We had two hundred extras for the day, and a camera crane — and at the end of the day, the director neglected to get the shot. I was so upset, that I've always said, 'One day, I'm going to have that shot!'

"So for 'Carrier', I wanted the audience to get the sense of — 'This is unpleasant; this is not something I want to happen to *me*; this is a danger; if this is what the 4400 can do, maybe Lytell and Barbara Yates and, ultimately, Ryland are right.' So we had two hundred extras lying there playing dead, and a camera crane. We started shooting in the diner and went out into the street. Scary stuff.

"And I finally got my shot."

characters on the screen was happening off the screen, too. It made perfect sense, so I used that for my character," Chad Faust says.

"I liked that we established Alana and Kyle with a friendship rather than as 'the new mom'," Katrina Lombard comments. "We didn't rehearse the underlying feelings; our reactions just came out while we were shooting. That's better than planning every move, because I believe a good actor will stop thinking the minute they say 'Action.' Thinking," she concludes with a big laugh, "is highly overrated!"

The audience learns several things about Kyle from Alana, including that his favorite food is meatloaf, and that his favorite writer is Alan Moore, well-known for his graphic novels *Watchmen*, *V for Vendetta* and *From Hell*. How is it that this writer, from among the millions possible, was picked? "If I had chosen one of my own favorite writers as Kyle's, it would have been William Faulkner or Samuel Beckett — and that would have sounded pretentious or ridiculous, and been all wrong," Ira Behr admits. "So Craig, who is closer to Kyle's age than I am, said, 'Alan Moore.' And since Alan Moore is the only graphic novelist that I would have accepted, I said okay."

The episode ends with Kyle feeling comfortable enough with Tom and Alana's vision of him to actually consider applying to medical school — only to have that pleasant moment shattered when his memory of murdering Jordan Collier unexpectedly surfaces. For Kyle, that memory is as horrific as the episode's opening image of a town full of dead people had been for the audience. And to peak the audience's anticipation about events about to unfold, the episode ends on a police sketch of the unknown killer, taped to the wall at NTAC. "The prop department had someone draw that sketch from photographs," Faust says. "I thought it was perfect, because it looked enough like me, but different enough to not be. Which was the purpose of it — to keep Tom guessing." O

Rebirth

Written by: Lisa Melamed
Directed by: Milan Cheylov

Guest Cast: Garret Dillahunt (Matthew Ross), Natasha Gregson Wagner (April Skouris), Kaj-Erik Eriksen (Danny Farrell), Chilton Crane (Susan Farrell), Kavan Smith (Garrity) with Luke Askew (Lee Kendall) and Hill Harper (Edwin Mayuya)

Kyle is afraid to reveal his involvement in Collier's murder to Tom, who's working the investigation. But Tom and Diana are briefly sidetracked when NTAC hears about several unexplained reversals of birth defects at a local hospital where a 4400 works as a nurse.

At the 4400 Center, Matthew Ross briefs Shawn about the same rumors. The returnee in question is Edwin Mayuya, a Rwandan emigrant who fled his country during the campaign to wipe out its Tutsi population. Ross feels that someone with the ability to repair genetic damage *in utero* would be an asset to the Center. Tom and Diana reach Mayuya first, and he agrees to submit to testing at NTAC if the agency will keep his identity under wraps. But Ross outs Mayuya to the media, believing that the revelation will be beneficial to the Center's cause.

Once Mayuya's face appears on television screens, all hell breaks loose. Edwin Mayuya is actually Edwin Musinga, a Hutu physician the Rwandan government has sought since 1995. He's accused of allowing the slaughter of hundreds of Tutsis at his medical clinic. Now the friends and relatives of those victims want revenge, and the Rwandan government demands his extradition.

The situation puts NTAC's two top agents at odds, with Tom firm in his belief that Musinga should be executed for his passive participation in the genocide, and Diana convinced that his abilities are so profound that Musinga could atone for his sins. Ultimately, the U.S. government decides to fight Musinga's extradition, but only *if* he continues to perform his miracles. However, tests on Musinga establish that those miracles are killing him. Each time he heals a fetus, his own genes mutate. He'll die within a year if he continues to heal the unborn. Since either choice equals a death sentence, Musinga accepts the sentence that will help others, and NTAC delivers him to the 4400 Center to live out his remaining days.

On the home front, Kyle's increasingly odd behavior inspires his cousin Danny to contact Shawn, with whom he's recently reconciled, for help. Shawn offers Kyle refuge at the Center to work out his problems, but Kyle opts for a different alternative — and disappears.

NTAC INFORMATION ARCHIVE

"The scene in 'Rebirth' where Shawn and Danny go to Kyle's house to invite him to the Center is the first scene that the three of us, Patrick, Kaj and I, have had together," Chad Faust points out. "The director, Milan Cheylov, was really good at bringing out the triangle of that scene. The beauty of acting on television is that you create a history to play off of, and we'd been doing it a lot by then, so we had plenty of that history. That's still one of my favorite scenes."

> **"Dad. I had to leave. I'm sorry." - Kyle**

"'I've got to be really honest about this," Joel Gretsch states. "When I read the script to 'Rebirth', I didn't understand it from my character's viewpoint. I thought, 'God, Tom's going to come off as such a hard ass.'"

To Gretsch, Tom's immediate anger toward Edwin Mayuya just didn't feel like the character he'd been building over the course of the series. So he scoured the script, searching for something that would justify Tom's deep antipathy. "The only thing I could hang Tom's hat on was his dialogue with Diana after the two of them have interviewed Edwin Mayuya. He says, "'It's great what he's doing now, but what was he doing back then?' That one speech saves me. The fact that this guy stood by while thousands of helpless people — children — were being massacred, enrages Tom. He just doesn't have the ability to accept that. And Joel doesn't either, to be honest. I'm not saying whether that emotional choice was the right one or the wrong one," Gretsch adds. "But at the time it allowed me to play that script. From the viewpoint of my character, that was my most difficult episode. The story touched on a big subject, and it never felt resolved."

"'Rebirth' presented an interesting dilemma," Craig Sweeny agrees. "It's the most naked social commentary we've done. But it was a little light on story, so it's the one show where Tom seems a little over the top in his anger."

Given the permutations the script went through, it's surprising that it conveyed a story at all. As showrunner, Ira Behr had intended the episode to be, if not a comedy, then at least something "lighter" than the average episode. "'Rebirth' started as the story of a Las Vegas singer who comes back with the ability to make people feel good about themselves," Behr explains. "But he discovers that the woman he loves has married a music big wig who has the master tapes to..." Behr

Above: Edwin Mayuya's (Hill Harper) past actions inspire a level of anger in Tom that surprises Diana.

Above: Worried about their cousin Kyle's odd behavior, brothers Shawn and Danny Farrell attempt a friendly intervention.

pauses with a shrug. "It *could* have been fun," he continues, taking a different tack. "But for some reason, and I'm totally serious about this, anything that's lighter just becomes a burden on this series. You don't know what tone you're looking for, or how far you can go. So, inevitably, you find that you can't do it. Which meant that we had to reach deep down to pull out something else."

"We'd lost four days breaking that story, and then a couple more days trying to plug in a new story," Fred Rappaport recalls. "I'd been pitching an idea about a 4400 who had returned, apparently depressed and uninterested in any news coverage. But it turns out that he had worked with Pol Pot [the ruthless leader of the *Khmer Rouge* movement, responsible for the deaths of over a million people in Cambodia's infamous 'killing fields']. He wasn't depressed and press shy — he was a former torturer. But Ira never liked it. Then Craig suggested the guy be from Rwanda, and gave the guy this ability to heal."

The fact that Mayuya can only cure birth defects in utero, "makes him different from Shawn," Behr points out. "And Hill Harper, who did a good job as Edwin, is one of the actors we knew from our initial auditions for the character of Richard Tyler."

The newest member of the repertory, Matthew Ross, plays a part in both the episode's A and B story. Not only does he alert the press to Mayuya's ability, but he also encourages Shawn to visit with his family. "Shawn was so disenfranchised at that point, that Matthew needed him to deal with it and heal himself," Garrett Dillahunt says, acknowledging that it's advice Matthew should take as well. "I don't think there was a lot of love in the Ross household as he grew up. So his idea of how to get things done is a little cold, even though they may be motivated for the right reasons."

Shawn's reunion results in a family dinner, which doesn't go the way either he or his mom had hoped. "When I read the dinner table scene, I remember thinking, 'Wow, that's really written hard,'" Kaj-Erik Eriksen says. "Before that, Danny hadn't been painted quite so angry and dark. So I tried to deliver the lines a little lighter, and it just didn't work. But once we started shooting it, all of a sudden Patrick upped the ante by bringing even more hostility into the scene. My reaction was, 'Well, if you're going to raise your voice to me, I'll raise mine back,' and we just played off of each other until I think you see real tension and conflict. It's great when that happens," Eriksen says with a smile. "It's what acting should be."

Above: In a gesture of reconciliation, Diana gives her departing sister April their mother's ring.

The episode closes one chapter in the lives of the Skouris family, as Diana surprises April at the bus station before the younger woman leaves town — and gives her the ring that she'd pawned. "Diana does love her sister," Jacqueline McKenzie says, "but she can be a little self righteous. She saw how happy April made Maia, and yet she says, 'I don't want you seeing my daughter anytime soon.' I think it's a trait that she doesn't really love in herself, which is one of the reasons she gives her the ring."

For Natasha Gregson Wagner, receiving such a sentimental gift solidifies the family. "The gesture says a thousand words," Wagner says. "April does things to get Diana's attention, because deep down inside she's worried that if she doesn't make herself known, she'll disappear. But she does things the wrong way. Now she's learned that Diana is gracious and generous.

"And I also feel that April's relationship to that ring has been redefined," Wagner concludes. "She'll certainly never pawn it again, that's for sure."

And the ring does resurface, along with April, during the show's third season. ⊙

Hidden

Written by: Frederick Rappaport
Directed by: Vincent Misiano

Guest Cast: Garret Dillahunt (Matthew Ross), Karina Lombard (Alana Mareva), Kaj-Erik Eriksen (Danny Farrell), Lindy Booth (Liv), Lexa Doig (Wendy Paulson), Richard Kahan (Marco Pacella), Kavan Smith (Garrity), Lori Triolo (Linda Baldwin)

As Jarvis senses that the agency is getting closer to Collier's killer, she pushes her agents harder. But both Diana and Tom have distractions at home. Maia's had a premonition that if the agents catch up with their prey, someone will get hurt. There are no specifics, but the heartfelt nature of the warning is enough to make Diana nervous.

Tom is following an investigation of his own, trying to track down Kyle. Most of his leads are cold, but he finds increasing evidence that Kyle took off because he was in serious trouble — and afraid to turn to Tom for help. Tom begins to fear that his search for Kyle and NTAC's search for Collier's assassin may be one and the same.

Danny visits his brother at the Center, and while he's there, meets ex-junkie Liv, who's been trying to straighten out her life by serving at the facility. Danny and Liv hit it off, and she sneaks out of the compound to accompany him to a party. While she's there, however, she yields to old habits and steals some pills. Back at the Center, a guard catches her with the goods, but Shawn decides to give her another chance.

Although ex-wife Linda said she had no clue as to Kyle's whereabouts, Tom suspects otherwise. Sure enough, Tom discovers that she's hidden him in a vacant house represented by her real estate agency. Tom confronts his son and learns *everything* — about the blackouts, the weapons he purchased and the carefully thought-out murder. Kyle is freaked out by his own behavior, but Tom is quick to reassure him that *he* wasn't responsible for his actions; the future people were controlling him. What's more, Tom doesn't intend to let Kyle go to jail. He puts together a plan for Alana to whisk his son out of the country. But before the pair can fly to Brussels, Jarvis alerts Tom and Diana that the police have captured their prime suspect — and it isn't Kyle.

Relieved, Tom tells Alana she can bring Kyle home. He's safe. But Tom is now burdened with a heavy secret.

Feeling as if she's literally dodged a bullet, Diana tells Maia she can stop worrying — it's all over. But Maia disagrees. It's not over… yet.

NTAC INFORMATION ARCHIVE

"I came up with the idea that Alana discovers Kyle's hiding place for the locker key," says Fred Rappaport. "And it really worked on paper, but the way it was shot makes no sense. Originally, Tom asks her how she knew, and she says that she remembered in the alternate universe that this was where Kyle hid things. Scott Peters argued at the time that everything in that alternate universe comes out of Tom's head, so why doesn't Tom remember? And I argued, 'Well, Tom forgot. It's an example of Tom not being as close to his son as he should be. Another thing for Tom to feel guilty about.' That was my argument. But I got overruled on it, and the scene got changed. Now it just implies that Alana knows Kyle better than Tom does."

> "A bodysnatching defense, Alana? I'm not sure the jury's gonna buy it." - Tom

"I think we may have focused a bit too much on '4400s of the week' and closed-ended episodes during the second season," Jeff Wachtel says. "But we adapted and began to focus more on how the characters interrelate in the big picture, and that proved to be truer to the soul of the show."

After having introduced a new 4400 in every episode with the

exception of 'As Fate Would Have It', the writers opted for another palate cleanser, a very straightforward police story. While it wasn't as big a change of pace as 'Life Interrupted', it was the team's first conscious effort to do a procedural. "And because of that," notes Ira Behr, "everyone, including me, got very nervous that it was going to end up being too dry. So we made sure to angst it up a lot — building to the big moment between Kyle and Tom."

"We all thought there would be great suspense in Tom trying to find Kyle, who he's come to suspect is Jordan's killer, while Diana and Nina are closing in on the killer — without knowing who it is," Fred Rappaport explains. "We wrote those parallel 'Can Tom find his son before they do?' scenes. But the first draft ended up being *too* much of a procedural, so we added the subplot of Maia warning her mother that someone — presumably Diana — was going to get hurt if the manhunt continued. Then it developed into a pretty good story."

But the plot threat based on Maia's premonition created a different problem — unexpected post-production angst for the producers. "For the scene with the wrong guy being arrested, we'd written that he actually kills a couple of cops when he shoots at Diana," Rappaport says. "The scene as initially shot really had impact, with the guy ranting and screaming like a psycho. The actor just went for it. But while it was being edited, Ira came up with the idea of giving Kyle a relationship with this guy's girlfriend. Which led us to realize that we couldn't demonize him as

Above: As efforts to find the fugitive who killed Jordan Collier intensify, Jarvis joins her agents in the hunt.

Above: Tom is relieved to find his son Kyle hiding in an empty house.

much as we had, because if he *did* kill a cop, he would *deserve* to go to jail — and that would reflect on the kind of girl that she must be. So we had to cut the scene up, taking out the parts where the bullets hit the cops. The scene hadn't been designed to be edited that way, which made it a bitch to recut. Plus, we had to mute all of the guy's screaming, so now the scene is silent and carries a lot less impact.

"That's what happens when you're serializing and you don't want to screw up future story," Rappaport notes with a shrug.

Pairing up Diana and Nina to search for Collier's assassin offered NTAC's two top females their first opportunity to work together. "My scenes very seldom take place out of the office," Samantha Ferris says, "so it was fun for me."

"The entire crew began saying, 'I smell spin-off,'" Jacqueline McKenzie jokes. "They loved seeing Sam and me together. She's a very funny woman. In fact, around her, *I* became the blushing damsel — and I'm an Aussie, so it takes a lot to make me blush!"

Another intriguing pairing brought up echoes of the first season. When Danny Farrell goes to the 4400 Center to speak his brother, Shawn introduces him to Liv, the beautiful waif that Shawn is helping to detox. "It seemed like an interesting

NTAC INFORMATION ARCHIVE

"I always have a couple of days worth of stubble when I'm playing Marco, because he's the kind of guy that you feel you're catching during his day off from shaving," Richard Kahan says. "It's strange, because on the one hand, Marco's not gonna be putting gel in his hair in the morning; he just doesn't have time to be concerned with stuff like that. And yet, on the other hand, he wears geek chic at it's finest, probably because we have the best wardrobe people on this show.

"But Marco has some style sense, and that's visible in the way he dresses in layers. He has shirts over shirts over shirts, and a blazer with letters and things sticking out of the pockets. But those blazers are great. I looked at one of the labels and it said 'Dolce & Gabbana', and I remember thinking, 'Wow, Marco must be doing better than I am!' Although I'm not going to lie, there's some elements of that in my personal wardrobe too, so I think it's great.

"Marco is young, but he's got a good paying government job, and he gets a company car. He doesn't have time to spend his money aside from sci-fi festivals and such, so I think he spends it on his wardrobe. And he wears fashionable, yet oversized glasses. So when you get into some of those duds, putting on those glasses really seals the deal. That's the key to who he is."

way to go, after what happened with Nikki," Behr says. "Nikki had a thing for Danny and then went for Shawn. Now Liv has a thing for Shawn, and goes for Danny. I kind of liked that."

Kaj-Erik Eriksen had reason to like it as well. "It's the first time during the season that they separated Danny's storyline from Kyle's and gave him one of his own," Eriksen points out. "That excited me, because things finally were looking up for my character. Go Danny! Of course, it wasn't long before he got screwed over again," he adds with a sigh.

In the end, the brothers reunite to wash Danny's car together, providing them with a nice bonding moment, "which I think was really important at that point," Behr says. But the showrunner had an even stronger image

Above: Marco Pacella (Richard Kahan) is eager to offer Diana his support — and more.

in mind. "The car washing scene was supposed to be fun and calming. But then the camera pulls back to show all the security guards standing watch over Shawn. That pull back was supposed to tell the audience, 'You're having fun, but you're having fun with one of the most important people in the world, so the fun is only illusionary.' Now, that's all there," Behr says, "but it just doesn't read. It worked great on the page, but when we looked at it, we all said, 'Well, that's not clear.' As Nietzsche said, 'Between the dream and the reality falls the shadow.'"

Two more pairings provided unexpected bonding moments. One gave Marco the opportunity to comfort Diana in a parking lot. "Marco was worried for Diana's safety," Richard Kahan says. "He was trying to tell her as a colleague that she should listen to Maia, and he was trying to tell her as a friend that he was concerned for her. The quiet strength of that scene is a tribute to Chris Misiano, who's directed many of our shows. It's still one of my favorite scenes. Plus, I got to hug Jacqui, which is always fun."

Finally, Tom and Kyle began the episode about as far apart as a father and son can be, both physically and psychologically. As Tom searches for his missing son, he's surprised to learn from Danny that he's been misreading Kyle for weeks, and from Wendy that Kyle may love him but doesn't trust him. Nevertheless, in the end, they too have an interesting rapprochement as they dispose of the gun used to kill Collier. "The idea of a father and son colluding together and throwing that weapon from a bridge is another bonding moment," Ira Behr states. "But it's a dark bonding moment." ○

Lockdown

Written by: Douglas Petrie
Directed by: Douglas Petrie

Guest Cast: Garret Dillahunt (Matthew Ross), Roger Cross (Major Culp), Jeffrey Combs (Kevin Burkhoff), Kaj-Erik Eriksen (Danny Farrell), Richard Kahan (Marco Pacella), Kavan Smith (Garrity) and Tom Verica (Dr Max Hudson)

O n the morning of Jordan Collier's birthday, every person at NTAC receives an email blaming the agency for Collier's death. Suddenly, the air at the facility resonates with an irritating high-pitched buzz. Although the women can't hear it, it triggers a pronounced reaction in the men, who begin exhibiting signs of barely suppressed rage. In minutes, tensions rise to such a fever pitch that one of the male agents shoots Jarvis.

Thanks to the homeopathic tranquilizers he's been popping to lower his anxiety level, Tom is calm enough to initiate a lockdown. Until someone figures out what's happening, no one will be able to get out — or in.

That's bad news for Diana, who desperately needs to get into the NTAC med lab, where Maia is being treated for a high fever and a mysterious rash. Unable to reach Tom, she calls Marco in the theory room. Like every other man in the building, Marco is experiencing his own version of 'roid rage', but he's already hard at work analyzing the triggering signal. Diana convinces him to find her a way into the building.

In the meantime, Tom and the other agents are held captive by the heavily-armed NSA soldiers that Jarvis recently brought onboard for security. Fearing that the soldiers might harm the 4400s in the med labs, Tom incapacitates a guard and grabs a gun. But he'll have to fight his way through an obstacle course full of half-crazed men en route, and the valerian is wearing off…

Diana barricades herself, Dr Hudson, Maia, Jarvis, and three female 4400s within NTAC's gymnasium. Hudson has stayed level with tranquilizer injections, but he's almost out. As the group waits inside the gym, they hear mayhem out in the corridors. But when the doors finally come crashing in, the crazed man wielding a gun at Diana is Tom!

Just as Diana is faced with the prospect of shooting her own partner, Hudson knocks him to the ground, and in the ensuing melee, Diana manages to incapacitate

NTAC INFORMATION ARCHIVE

Baby Isabelle has always been closest to her mother, Lily, but in 'Lockdown' Richard realizes that she is finally talking to him. "It was almost like a rivalry," Laura Allen says. "I didn't know where Isabelle's loyalties were, so she was a force to deal with."

"During the middle of the second season, we were concerned because Ali's character, Richard, was out of the loop," Ira Behr explains. "But by the time we got to 'Lockdown', we were playing a whole bunch of things, and one of them was that baby Isabelle was going to be the strongest of those characters. So we got the idea that the baby knows Lily is having second thoughts about the Center, and the baby also knows that she has to be there because that's where the action is. And since that's where Richard is, we had her start sending her love to Richard."

Tom. Suddenly, a strange sound fills the air. When Hudson visibly relaxes, Diana realizes that Marco has figured out a way to neutralize the killer signal.

The crisis averted, the agents realize they have only two things to worry about: Maia's condition has deteriorated — and T.J. Kim, one of the three female 4400s, is missing. The perpetrator of the deadly attack has gotten away.

> "Look, I just gave you permission to blow my head off. Why don't you call me Max?" - Dr Hudson

"'Lockdown' was a kind of prelude to the two-parter that would wrap up the season," relates Craig Sweeny. The writers toyed with having the episode involve a terrorist attack launched by a 4400. "But beyond that, we didn't know what it would be," Sweeny continues. "And then I saw *Battle Royale*."

Based on a novel by Koushun Takami, *Battle Royale* is a violent cinematic tale of the near future in which Japan's adults opt to solve the problem of increasingly nihilistic teenagers by sending the delinquents to an isolated island. There, the teens are told they must eliminate each other in combat — or be blown up. "It's such a wacky movie, I thought Sweeny would like it," Fred Rappaport confesses. "So I loaned him a copy."

"It inspired me," says Sweeny. "These kids were pitted against each other in a battle for survival. It was like a hyper-violent *Lord of the Flies*. It gave me the concept

Above: NOVA assassin T.J. Kim (far right) wasn't Leanne Adachi's first role on *The 4400*. The actress had appeared as an unnamed nurse in the episode 'White Light'.

Above: It's not polite to point. The intense situation almost destroys a solid friendship.

for 'Lockdown' — with everyone trapped inside NTAC trying to kill each other."

Although *Battle Royale* is a top grossing Japanese film as well as an international cult classic, the film has inspired intense debate in its homeland over media violence. Not surprisingly, 'Lockdown' triggered similar qualms at USA Network. "It was supposed to be a real rock 'em sock 'em action adventure," notes Ira Behr. "But we had to cut back on the violence, even a lot of the implied violence." The changes, Behr feels, watered down the episode's intent. "The way I see it, you either commit to a story or you don't," he sighs.

On the other hand, a secondary inspiration worked out rather well, Sweeny comments. "We'd decided that within this story of a terrorist attack we'd give something cool to Diana. That led to having Maia coincidentally be at NTAC, so Diana would have to protect her in this dangerous environment." The touchstone for this scenario was the film *Aliens*, where Sigourney Weaver's character, Ripley, fights to protect the young girl, Newt. "That's when it turned into the 'badass Diana' episode," Sweeny grins.

Jacqueline McKenzie tackled the situation with relish, despite a few handicaps. For one thing, as the season wound down, much of the series' rapidly dwindling budget was allocated to the all-important final two episodes. And that meant cutting corners on 'Lockdown'.

"Diana tries to get into NTAC and there's only *one* security guard stopping her," groans Behr. "*One* guy. That's where you could really see there was no money."

"Yeah, we got to that scene and [director] Doug Petrie told me, 'You can't get in.'

NTAC INFORMATION ARCHIVE

"The theory room isn't a very big set, so there aren't a lot of camera angles or different shots that can physically happen in there," Richard Kahan comments. "A big part of shooting in the theory room is that everyone has had their time to be in front of the projector. There's a screen in the back of the room that's constantly showing projected images, like maps or the work that Marco and his team are working on. And we've found that we each have had a turn at standing in front of that screen and having the eerie light of the projector shine on our faces as we act. Every new director tries to find new ways to shoot in there, which is always interesting, but essentially, we've done many similar-looking scenes."

I said, 'What do you mean I can't get in? There's only one dude here,'" McKenzie chuckles. "So he said, 'There are helicopters above.' But there obviously weren't. So I told him, 'You'd better remember to put in helicopter sounds, mate.'"

McKenzie's other handicap was manmade — specifically, Joel Gretsch-made. For the scene where Diana and Tom square off against one another, weapon to weapon, the actors were provided with real guns, sans ammunition, which are relatively heavy given that they have to be held at arm's length for extended periods of time.

"You hold the gun up for blocking," Gretsch says. "And lighting. And set-up. And then for the first take. And then another. It's heavy. And it gets heavier. So after each take they'd yell 'Cut,' and Jacqui would go, '*Uh!*'" Gretsch grunts an approximation of the sound. "So while we were doing that scene, I rested my gun *on top* of hers, making hers even heavier," Gretsch says, a wicked gleam in his eyes. "So she's going '*Uh!*' and I'm just dying.

"But the great thing about Jacqui is she uses stuff like that," Gretsch adds. "She's an actor's actor, and she's always looking for moments that are *real*. So by then we were *having* that moment, and what was *real* was that her arm was killing her. And as I pushed down a little harder, she was right at the breaking point — and the camera was taking that all in."

"It was method Joel," comments McKenzie, "so I just accepted it as part of that. He was grinning the whole time, doing what Tom would do in the moment, tantalizing and aggressing Diana," she says. "Then they called 'Cut' and he was Joel again."

The episode also provided some good moments for supporting characters Kevin Burkhoff and Marco Pacella. Jeffrey Combs' Burkhoff got the plum opportunity to tell the world that he thinks the folks at the 4400 Center are pulling off a scam. "We needed someone to say that," notes Behr. "Kevin was the obvious choice. He's too crazy *not* to speak the truth. Children and madmen will always tell you the skinny, that the Emperor has no clothes."

And speaking of madmen, Richard Kahan was delighted to portray "Mad Marco", as the cast referred to him. "It's fun to play the other side of a character," the actor says. "Raising his voice to Diana and the guys in the theory room was way out of character, even though Marco didn't get nearly as aggressive as the other NTAC guys. The signal that T.J. Kim sends out seemed to focus directly on men's testosterone levels, so I guess the implication was that Marco is more 'sensitive' than the others," Kahan conjectures. "That allowed him to maintain his composure enough to help Diana out. It says a lot about Marco."

And what does it say about Tom Baldwin that he also managed to hang on to his sanity longer than the other guys? That the homeopathic valerian tablets he was taking helped him to stay mellow? "No," Gretsch says with a laugh. "It may sound ridiculous, but I believe what gave 'Wonderman Tom' his resilience is that Tom's the hero of the show." O

Written by: Ira Steven Behr & Craig Sweeny
Directed by: Scott Peters

Guest Cast: Peter Coyote (Dennis Ryland), Garret Dillahunt (Matthew Ross), Karina Lombard (Alana Mareva), Jeffrey Combs (Kevin Burkhoff), Richard Kahan (Marco Pacella), Andrew Airlie (Brian Moore), Keegan Connor Tracy (Alison Driscoll), Harris Allan (Sam Marsden) and Tom Verica (Dr Max Hudson)

NTAC receives reports that 4400s all over the world have contracted the same malady that's affecting Maia. Initially characterized by a rash and a high fever, the illness affects the returnees' immune systems, leaving them vulnerable to all manner of diseases. It also nullifies any abilities they may have.

With Nina Jarvis still out of commission, NTAC's D.C. office puts Dennis Ryland in temporary command of the Seattle division. But Ryland's loyalties are to his bosses, not to the returnees that Tom and Diana want to protect. Ryland issues orders requiring *all* 4400s, sick or well, to report to quarantine. If they don't come in voluntarily, he states, NTAC will bring them in.

Many healthy returnees balk at the order, but no one denies the seriousness of the illness, which has stricken one in five returnees. Even Shawn has been incapacitated. He passes temporary leadership of the Center to Richard, who must work with Ross to come up with a strategy that addresses Ryland's decree.

As Dr Hudson continues to treat Maia, Diana notices that her daughter's medical chart seems to have been tampered with. First she notices that a page is missing, then, after the page reappears, she sees that certain information has been blacked out. NTAC isn't making any progress in analyzing the disease, so Diana decides to contact Kevin Burkhoff, the recovered neuroscientist who knows more than anyone about 4400 technology. But Hudson refuses to share the classified files Burkhoff needs for his research, so Diana must convince Marco to obtain them.

Ryland leads a squad of NTAC agents to the Center to gather those 4400s who've refused to report to quarantine, but discovers they're gone. Richard has relocated them to a safe house where he vows he'll protect them. But Lily, concerned for Isabelle's safety, doesn't want to stay there. She trusts neither NTAC nor the staff at the Center, which has been following Collier's old agenda by running tests on the baby without her permission. Feeling she has no other choice, she contacts her ex-husband Brian and flees in the middle of the night with Isabelle.

It doesn't take Burkhoff long to figure out what's killing the returnees. It's not a disease — it's a side effect! Apparently, the scientists at NTAC have been dosing the 4400s with a synthetic substance they call a "promicin inhibitor" at every single government-mandated checkup; the dosage is referenced on page five of each patient's medical report. Now this inhibitor has turned deadly.

NTAC has brought the 4400 to the brink of death!

> "We did it to them, Tom. We made them sick." - Diana

"I had been reading about the Tuskegee Experiment," Craig Sweeny says. "Making

the 4400 sick came loosely from that case."

In that government-sanctioned atrocity, the US Public Health Service intentionally withheld treatment from 399 black men infected with syphilis over a forty-year period in order to collect data from their eventual autopsies — an act that President Clinton later condemned as "deeply, profoundly, morally wrong."

Which is exactly the reaction that Diana has when she realizes the truth and delivers the episode's last line of dialogue, "We made them sick."

As the returnees around the world begin to show symptoms of an unknown ailment, Dr Kevin Burkhoff shows up at NTAC to offer his research notes to Dr Max Hudson. "Originally, Hudson was supposed to be a love interest for Diana," Ira Behr reveals. "But we didn't see any chemistry between them, so it didn't go anywhere. But Tom Verica [*American Dreams*] is a really good actor, so we brought him into the promicin scandal in the later episodes."

"The writers told me that Hudson would be a love interest," Jacqueline McKenzie says. "But I never saw an opportunity for that to happen, because basically I met him when Maia was hospitalized, and I couldn't see flirting with him over my dying, sick child."

"I don't think that Kevin trusted Hudson for a second," Jeffrey

Above: Dr Kevin Burkhoff (Jeffrey Combs) accepts NTAC records from an extremely nervous Marco.

NTAC INFORMATION ARCHIVE

Viewers with sharp eyes — or a pause button — and a bit of knowledge about film work may have noticed that as Diana flips through Maia's hospital chart, not only is page five missing, but page three actually is the back side of a 'call sheet', the production's daily list of shots, personnel and times to report for make-up, etc.

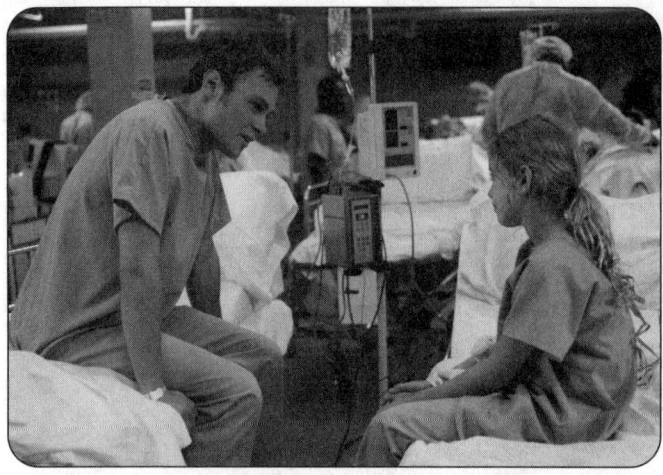

Above: Although the actors were well acquainted, 'The Fifth Page' offered the first scene that Patrick Flueger and Conchita Campbell acted in together.

Combs says. "He imagines that if the patients are getting their physicals from these doctors, then these doctors are in league with NTAC. He plays a bit of chess with Hudson when he says, 'I've shown you mine, so now you show me yours.' Of course, Hudson won't reciprocate, so Kevin catches him. That's why Kevin feels such disdain.

"But I think Kevin was beginning to trust Tom and Diana," Combs continues. "They weren't sure about him, because everybody sees him as a bit of an oddball, so whatever he says has to be taken with a grain of salt. But once again, Kevin is ahead of the curve here, so he challenges them to open their eyes to the facts."

Although viewers had no reason to suspect that Burkhoff was doing research on the 4400, no one was surprised when he showed up. "Kevin dances to a different drummer, and while the rest of us are thinking about what to have for dinner, he's working on high calculus or complex equations," Combs notes. "He's probably a social misfit, a bit of a hermit, and unable to work on a normal level. He's never been what you and I would perceive as normal. In fact, I don't think that Kevin's normal is your normal or my normal."

Which is why Burkhoff is the only person outside of NTAC who's able to figure out that the returnees' abilities come from a substance called promicin.

The first symptoms from the promicin inhibitor appear as a skin rash — one that had to be carefully applied by the make-up department. On a normal day, Conchita Campbell spends a minimum amount of time in the make-up chair "for a little lip balm and stuff under my eyes," Campbell says. "But I loved being there, and I used to say, 'Oh, I wish I could sit in the make-up chair longer like Joel or Jacqui.'" Then one day, she got her wish. "I was sitting in the chair before I knew they were going to put the rash on me. So when the make-up lady started to paint those little dots on my arm, I said, 'Oh, this is so much fun.' But after a couple of days, I was like,

NTAC INFORMATION ARCHIVE

In 'The Fifth Page', a sick and mournful Alana tells Tom, 'I always hoped we'd get married for real in this world." Although there's no follow up scene in the aired episode, there is one in the script. Tom fulfills Alana's wish by bringing a minister to the quarantine facility and the two are married. The scene was cut for time.

'Okay, that's enough.' It only took a half hour, but as she was painting, my arm would get stiff, but I couldn't move it because it might make her mess up. I had to fight against the need to move my arm."

When many of the sick 4400, including Shawn and Maia, gather in quarantine, Campbell got another of her wishes. "That was the first time that Patrick and I worked together on camera," she points out. "It was so much fun, because ever since the 'Pilot' we really loved to play together. Patrick was always going up to

Above: When he and Diana discover that Ryland is behind the promicin inhibitor scandal, Tom turns his back on a friendship that spans decades.

Scott Peters and saying, 'Okay, when are Conchita and I going to be together in a scene?' So we finally got it."

When Dennis Ryland and the NTAC agents raid the 4400 Center in order to apprehend the outstanding returnees, the facility is deserted — except for Matthew Ross. "I was the only one standing there," Garret Dillahunt says with a smile. "It was kind of cool that I was going down with the ship, so to speak. That's what got me to thinking that maybe Matthew's kind of a good guy. He does things differently than I might, but he's playing on a larger scale and is one of those guys who has an acceptable body count."

"Part of Ira's plan was to bring back Ryland," Fred Rappaport says. "Everything Tom believed in that Ryland represented suddenly gets torn asunder. It's Writing 101," Rappaport notes, donning his writer hat. "It's making the disease work for us on a personal level for each of the characters. The disease is the wedge that pushes Tom toward going against NTAC, because of what's happening with Alana. And it's the wedge that pushes Diana that way because of what's happening to Maia. The ones they love the most were screwed over — and by a man that Tom loves, his mentor, Ryland."

"Ending the season with Tom taking sides with the 4400 was a smart move," Rappaport concludes. "The 'Pilot' began with Tom having left NTAC because of his son. Now, after an entire season of getting back into his bosses' good graces, he goes against them at the end. That's very clever. It bookends both the season and the series." ○

Mommy's Bosses

Written by: Ira Steven Behr & Craig Sweeny

Directed by: John Behring

Guest Cast: Peter Coyote (Dennis Ryland), Garret Dillahunt (Matthew Ross), Karina Lombard (Alana Mareva), Jeffrey Combs (Kevin Burkhoff), Richard Kahan (Marco Pacella), Andrew Airlie (Brian Moore), Keegan Connor Tracy (Alison Driscoll), Tom Verica (Dr Max Hudson) and Billy Campbell (Jordan Collier)

Tom and Diana begin rounding up rogue 4400s. Learning that seven returnees passed away during the night, they head for quarantine where they find that Alana is so sick she doesn't recognize the man she loves and Maia is going downhill fast.

Diana comes to a decision. Leading Tom to Max Hudson's office, she points her gun at the doctor's head, demanding to know who at NTAC ordered the use of the promicin inhibitor. Hudson seems relieved to reveal what he knows. He was the one who discovered, after Orson Bailey revealed his telekinetic abilities, that each of the 4400s has an extra neurotransmitter in their brains. Hudson guessed that it was this substance, which he named promicin, that gave Bailey his abilities — and could give the other returnees abilities of their own. Alarmed, Ryland's bosses in D.C. ordered Hudson to develop a drug that would suppress promicin production in the 4400. The unexpected result: hundreds of dying returnees.

Tom and Diana learn that every bit of paperwork related to promicin, the inhibitor and the abilities that some returnees developed despite the regular injections of the inhibitor, has vanished from NTAC's files. They have no proof of the conspiracy Hudson hinted at.

At the 4400 Center, Kevin Burkhoff has been researching promicin. Ross decides it would be a good idea for him to continue his work at the safe house where Richard is holed up. When Burkhoff reveals that he needs to find a 4400 who hasn't been exposed to the inhibitor, Richard realizes that Isabelle is the only person who fits that description. Now, if only he can get Lily to return with the baby...

But Isabelle is way ahead of him. She hasn't been happy since Lily took her away from Richard. After enduring a series of horrifying delusions caused by the not-so-helpless toddler, Lily breaks down and asks Brian to take her back to the safe house, giving Burkhoff access to the pure promicin in Isabelle's body.

Diana learns that Hudson has been found dead in his car, an apparent suicide. But he's left behind one last clue: a note to Diana saying only "Find the Firewall memo". After Marco reveals that Ryland always dictated his memos to his now-retired secretary Jane Orman, Diana and Tom head for Orman's house — and find her eager to talk to them. Jane still has a copy of the top-secret memo titled "Operation Firewall", ordering Hudson to begin injecting 4400s with the untested inhibitor. It's the smoking gun with Ryland's fingerprints all over it — and the signatures of people all the way up the governmental chain of command.

Although Ryland threatens to reveal Kyle's involvement in Jordan Collier's murder if Tom doesn't back down, Kyle tells Tom that he intends to turn himself in. Thus, Tom is free to use his knowledge of Operation Firewall to stop Ryland from taking the remaining 4400s by force. Ryland backs down — and is soon arrested for

Above: Given the likely alternative, Dr Max Hudson (Tom Verica) tells the agents all about the promicin inhibitor.

his involvement in the conspiracy.

Burkhoff succeeds in creating a serum from Isabelle's blood that neutralizes the inhibitor. He could only draw enough blood to create one dose — but one dose is enough to cure Shawn, who is then able to cure other sick people in quarantine.

Before Kyle turns himself in to the police, he visits the recovering Shawn and confesses that he killed Collier while under the influence of some strange future entity. Shawn reaches out, ostensibly to embrace him, but suddenly he seems to be drawing the life from Kyle. Shawn tells his dying cousin that he is freeing him — and suddenly a ball of energy emerges from Kyle and explodes! He is finally rid of the killing influence within him.

Later, as Tom walks Kyle up the courthouse steps, Lily frantically searches her suite at the Center for baby Isabelle, who's disappeared from her crib. In another suite, Shawn looks up from his newspaper to see a beautiful young woman standing naked in front of him. The woman introduces herself as "Isabelle". In another part of the Center, Kevin Burkhoff injects himself with a syringe of promicin. And on the shores of Highland Beach, a weary castaway finds himself in surprisingly familiar territory. It's Jordan Collier.

At Diana's apartment, she celebrates by sharing a romantic meal with Marco, but the mood changes when Maia reveals that nothing is over; "the war" has just begun.

> **"Nothing's over. It's just starting. The war." - Maia**

"Too many notes," Austria's Emperor Joseph II reportedly commented about some of Mozart's works. But as Mozart probably countered, every one of those notes was imperative. Which helps to explain why Ira Behr pushed for all those cliffhangers in the season two finale for *The 4400*.

"I have to admit I was worried about all those endings, although Ira wasn't," says Fred Rappaport. There were seven in all. Viewers would see six: Ryland being led away from NTAC in handcuffs; Burkhoff injecting himself with his first dose of promicin; Richard realizing he's developed an ability — telekinesis; Tom taking Kyle to the courthouse; Lily searching frantically for baby Isabelle — who shows up at Shawn's door as a fully grown woman; a disheveled, disoriented Jordan Collier appearing on Highland Beach.

"I thought there might be too many, that it would overload the audience," Rappaport admits. "But Ira just said, 'Let's go for the gusto.' He was in love with every single one. When he heard there was some concern, he sat down and looked at all of them. And on each one, he said, 'This is *great*.' Even the one with Billy Campbell and that big beard. Someone asked, 'Is anybody outside of the hardcore audience going to understand who the hell he is?' And all Ira would say was, 'So what?'"

In fact, the producers had decided months earlier that they wanted the scene with Campbell, so they shot it during 'As Fate Would Have It', Campbell's final episode before he left on his year-long voyage.

"Before 'As Fate Would Have It', I mentioned to Scotty [Peters] that when I returned I would have super long hair and a big honkin' gnarly beard — maybe they would want to use that in the show?" Campbell recalls. "Scotty went for the idea immediately, and got the okay from the network. I figured they'd let me do one episode looking like this homeless person, and then they'd say, 'Okay, now clean him up to the way he looked before he left.' But they really loved the idea. They said, 'Don't change a thing! In fact, make it worse. Put more grease in his beard!'"

"We took Billy out to Bunsen Lake on a second unit day," says Scott Peters, who directed Campbell's cliffhanger. At the time, Campbell had short hair and a neatly trimmed beard. "Our hair and make-up people made him look like Jesus," chuckles Peters. "That wasn't our intention, but..." Apparently it's hard to banish the 'J.C.' connection once you've got it in your head.

In addition to the footage on the beach, Peters also shot footage of Collier living in a woodland shack that was never used. "The producers thought better of it," notes Campbell. "They decided that it would be best to just let people wonder what I'd been doing."

One cliffhanger that appears in the script failed to make it into the final cut of 'Mommy's Bosses'. A Washington bureaucrat, one of several who've been indicted along with Ryland for involvement in the promicin scandal, is sitting alone in his office. As a clerk wheels a mail cart past the office, the bureaucrat rubs his ear, puzzled, as if he's heard something strange. The clerk keeps walking — it's T.J. Kim

— and viewers who've seen 'Lockdown' can guess what's about to happen.

The scene was dropped, but Kim soon would have the opportunity to wreak her revenge; she returns as part of the Nova Group in season three.

Although Ryland ends the second season as a man who's broken trust with his friends, one can almost understand where he's coming from. "As cold as Ryland is, he's not just some villain wearing a handlebar moustache," notes Rappaport. "There's rationale for why he acted the way he did. He wasn't doing it

Above: Ryland's motivations may have been understandable, but his actions were reprehensible.

for personal gain. He states his case eloquently, and I have to give Ira a cheer for letting him do that."

"Ryland thought he was doing the right thing," confirms Peter Coyote. "He didn't think of himself as a bad guy. Of course, Hitler probably didn't either. But little by little, what might have begun as a positive train of thought leads right on out to the horror. The thing I like most about Ryland is that he's always human. He's just arguing against a point of view that he thinks is careless. It's dangerous to be so cavalier about the fate of the Earth when you don't really know what's going on. Of course, as the show moves into the third season, he really does move beyond the pale."

While the revelation of Ryland's behavior, and that of his bosses in D.C., hits Tom the hardest, it also shakes up Diana. "I could imagine her terror," says Jacqueline McKenzie. "The fact that this took place, it's such a betrayal, not just of the 4400, but of everything. Diana doesn't know who she's working for anymore. These are the people that she's been dotting her 'i's and crossing her 't's for. The scandal aligns her much closer to Tom's point of view. In the future she'll be more willing to trust her instincts, like Tom."

All of this betrayal bears out what the more off-center individuals like Kevin Burkhoff have felt all along. "It's everything that Kevin has always feared about the government," explains Jeffrey Combs. "And it's a beautiful metaphor. All good sci-fi holds a mirror up to what's going on in the real world. And I think that the NTAC conspiracy stuff is not too far from what we're experiencing in the present day — our uncertainty over whether or not we can trust our government, our unwillingness to let the government encroach into our private lives. Not too much of a stretch there." O

Tom Baldwin

"If you're holding out any hope of keeping this cover-up, you're gonna have to start by putting me in the ground right here and now."

Tom Baldwin: Age forty-one. Lead investigator. On leave of absence from NTAC from August 2001 through August 2004. Wife Linda filed for divorce in 2004, after nineteen years of marriage. Entrusted by the future to help protect the 4400 and fulfill their mission of preventing a global catastrophe. Season two home address: 240 Parkside Ave., Seattle, WA 98117. — season two production notes

"Tom is a meat and potatoes kind of guy," states Joel Gretsch matter-of-factly. "He trusts his instincts and he acts. He's factual. So when this comet drops off 4400 people, his whole world turns upside down." Perhaps best known to audiences from his performances in two high profile Steven Spielberg-associated science fiction productions — *Taken* and *Minority Report* — Gretsch wasn't exactly eager to try out for *The 4400*. "I'd heard it was a sci-fi situation, so I wasn't enthusiastic," he admits. "Sci-fi can have a stigma to it. People will tell you they're not 'sci-fi fans', ignoring the fact that it can be a great setting for storytelling. But my agent encouraged me and said, 'It's a good read,' so I looked at the script and I immediately liked it. It was very gripping and really grounded in human drama. It had something that's very basic to me: the relationship with his son. Here's this comet about to hit Earth, and everybody leaves the hospital, even the doctors and nurses go to say goodbye to their loved ones. But Tom stays. In fact, there was this scene in the original script where he's desperately trying to find a battery pack because the ventilator that's keeping his son alive is running low on battery strength. And I just thought, 'God, somebody had the idea to write that.' I loved that this emotional moment was in there, and I figured that there was going to be really good storytelling here."

"Tom's the perfect model for the characters we wanted to portray on the show," notes Scott Peters. "He's the lead character and he's got a job to do, but his world is also centered around the fact that his son has been in a coma for three years. He's invested in both areas. We wanted to show these people away from their jobs, see who they were and who their families were, but between the procedural stuff and the home stuff, that can be a tough balance to strike. With Tom, we could see right away that it could be an organic thing; his home life didn't seem like a tacked-on subplot."

"We knew that with all the story elements we'd given to Tom — the son in a

coma, the nephew coming back, his sister, his ex-wife — that there'd be a lot of stuff bubbling in a cauldron," elaborates Ira Steven Behr. "But we'd written him as a very straight ahead guy. Very linear in his thinking: ABCDE, as opposed to Diana's outside-the-box ABECF kind of thinking. But as Joel played him, we started realizing that Tom was a guy with some anger management issues, a little more tormented than we had thought, a little more interesting. Joel really brought a lot of that to the table. He's a very deceptive actor. You think you know who he is because he's this good-looking guy with all-American features, but there are depths there that can take the audience by surprise. It's just been a pleasure watching him bring in this stuff that enables us to keep digging deeper into his character."

Yves Simoneau, Gretsch's director in the two-hour 'Pilot', had a similar take on the actor. "What I liked about Joel was that he could be very threatening in one second and very charming in the next," he explains. "Vulnerable and at the same time very solid. I knew that if the show went forward, this character was going to have to face tough situations, and I wanted to make sure that was believable when he pulled out a gun. But at the same time, because of his son, I wanted to make sure that he could let down his guard so the emotions could come out. And that's exactly what Joel offered. He has that capacity of going from one state to another without losing either his manhood or his sensitivity."

As the character that's had the most impact upon Tom Baldwin, no one appreciates Gretsch's abilities more than Chad Faust. "There's a lot of Joel in Tom," he reports. "He's one of the most loving people I know. And he's a real trooper. There's this pivotal scene in 'Trial by Fire' where Kyle — the other Kyle — is sitting under the sprinklers in the middle of the night and he tells Tom that he's not his son. But Joel was sick that day, and they told me I'd have to do my lines with the

script supervisor reading Tom's lines from off-camera," Faust recalls. "I was concerned, because Joel and I had made a real connection that we were using for our characters. But he came in and did the scene, even though he was under the weather."

Although the relationship between father and son is one of Gretsch's favorite things about the role, he initially found one aspect of it a bit disconcerting. "When we started the show, I had this one-and-a-half-year-old daughter at home," he relates, "so I wasn't sure how to play dad to this guy who I felt was my contemporary! Chad Faust — he's a man! He's not a baby. I'm too young to have a son that's that old. Well, biologically I'm *not*, actually," he chuckles, "but Joel had a hard time with that. I had to find this whole back history that wasn't in the script in order to home in on my character. What was my relationship with Kyle like prior to the coma? Why am I sitting there at his bedside alone and

why is the relationship with my wife having problems and why isn't she there with me? The writers gave me snippets of ideas but I had to fill them in for myself. I wrote up this whole backstory for myself — that she got pregnant, and we got married. That made Kyle's age make more sense to me. So we started this family, and I immersed myself in my work. Everything became about my work. I thought my family life would just be taken care of, and I wasn't a very good father or husband. The intensity of what Tom does can be consuming. And so I loved the fact that the overall scope of the show seemed to mirror Tom's life and the mistakes that he's made in the past. Here's a guy whose son is in a coma and he doesn't know how he got that way. He's so helpless. That does things to a marriage, creates cracks. You love your child so much that the cracks gets deeper and deeper until it finally severs."

He pauses to reflect on Tom's other major relationship, with partner Diana Skouris. Initially, that relationship doesn't seem very stable either. "Tom thinks of himself as a loner," Gretsch states. "Doesn't need anybody else, doesn't trust anybody else. Trust is a big issue for Tom. Always was, always will be. And continues to be as the show goes on, at least with his employers. With Diana, not so much. They both have a tendency to go their own way when the situation calls for it — and occasionally, to lie to each other — but they're always there for each other in the clinches."

The same can be said of Gretsch's commitment to the show and his co-workers. "It's a rare occasion, and I mean this with all sincerity, when you can honestly say, 'This is a good show with good people,'" he says fondly. "When you've been around long enough to know, and worked with enough crews and producers and cast members, it's nice to be able to say that. I love these people. We're like 'the little show that could' because every single person's intention is to do well and come back for another season. It just doesn't happen all that often, so I'm very happy." ○

"Whatever's coming through that door, I'll protect you."

Diana Skouris: Early thirties. NTAC agent. Ex-CDC [Center for Disease Control & Prevention] agent. Estranged from father. Partnered with Tom Baldwin when he returned to work in August 2004. Single, loner, uncharacteristically took Maia Rutledge into her home and later adopted her. Lives at 100 East Cordova Street, #312, Seattle, WA 98104. — season two production notes

While her persona on *The 4400* may seem the epitome of cool, collected self-confidence, the woman behind Diana Skouris is more prone to the occasional *faux pas*. A case in point: "I was sitting in this large room waiting to audition for the show," recalls Jacqueline McKenzie. "It was a shared area; they were also auditioning people for a show called *Blind Date*. And in walks this guy wearing the brightest, loudest Hawaiian shirt I've ever seen. He stood there, with his back against the wall, not saying anything. Well, I knew they were only auditioning girls for *The 4400* that day, so I figured he'd come in to try out for *Blind Date*. And I said to him, 'Wow, that's a nice shirt. You'll really get them with that.'"

The deadpan comment didn't elicit a response, and McKenzie forgot about it until she stepped into the audition room ten minutes later. "And there he was, with some of the producers. And suddenly I thought, 'Oh, my God...'" It was Ira Behr, showrunner for *The 4400* and aficionado of brightly colored shirts... and beards. But contrary to her fears, McKenzie did not blow the audition. She did, however, remain a bit leery of approaching him again for some time. "Then Ira came to the set while we were shooting '[The New and Improved] Carl Morrissey'," she chuckles, "and all I could think was 'Oh, my God, it's that *guy*...'"

To McKenzie's friends and admirers, the "cute-meet" with Behr is pretty typical behavior. The loquacious Australian is known as one of the friendliest people on *The 4400* set. "She's the one who holds our group together," confirms Kaj-Erik Eriksen. "Jacqui is always planning things for everybody to do on the weekend, and organizing the cast to go out for dinner."

"She knows how to be a great hostess who makes everybody feel a part of things," enthuses Natasha Gregson Wagner. "The minute you meet her she disarms you by being so nice."

"I just adore Jacqui," says Peter Coyote. "We're sort of dinner partners whenever I'm working, and we have so much fun. She's irreverent and funny and she just makes the long days zip by."

"Whenever we're done filming our scenes, we always play," laughs Conchita Campbell. "Jacqui's just a great person, caring and loving. We've become good friends."

None of which, of course, would be important if McKenzie weren't also a consummate actor who takes her job as seriously as her alter ego. "Jacqui *is* Diana while she's at work," Scott Peters states. "The same kind of no-nonsense character. And like Diana, when you get her home, she becomes a regular person. She has that charm and that endearing quality that makes you want to know what she's like underneath."

"She's totally there for the work, but she makes you feel comfortable to do *your* work," comments Wagner. "That's very appreciated."

McKenzie expects her fellow actors to be as prepared as she is for each and every scene. "I know it sounds pathetic," she says, "but I love to work with people who always know their lines, who are personally committed to the role and the backstory. That's all I want. You don't want someone just phoning it in — and that *can* happen."

McKenzie's portrayal of Skouris projects that attitude loud and clear, starting with the 'Pilot'. "Diana's very *cautious* when she's partnered with Tom," the actress says thoughtfully. "But I wouldn't say she's *antagonistic* towards him. She does things by the book. *He's* the antagonistic one, walking off the job and disappearing without telling anyone. Diana has crossed every 't' and dotted every 'i' in order to get a place of strength in her world. So she thinks Tom's a complete liability — and so does Dennis Ryland, which is why he calls Tom back into the field with great regret. Tom takes risks, great risks, and my character was not up for that. But over time, I think

Diana's learned that it doesn't matter how 'by the book' you do your job — because nobody else is doing it by the book!" She chuckles. "So ultimately, Diana learns from Tom."

It was, of course, the writers who moved Diana forward on the emotional evolutionary path. It didn't happen all at once, of course, but they'd had it in their minds from the beginning. "Diana's backstory wasn't activated at the time of the first few episodes," notes Robert Hewitt Wolfe. "It becomes more important as Maia becomes part of her life. But we really wanted to establish her first as a professional — someone who has never had a kid or thinks about the baggage with her family. We wanted to show that she was up for the task of working with Tom. I mean, obviously Diana has lots of character stuff and issues, but establishing Tom's backstory at the beginning was so important that it didn't leave us much room for Diana's stuff."

"She goes from being a character who's kind of interesting, who can think outside of the box but is a little too removed and a little too analytical, to being the guardian and mother of this strange child," interjects Ira Behr. "Which forces her to be the person that, for whatever reason, had been put aside in her life and in her prior relationships."

It is Maia's importance in her life, of course, that brings Diana more in sync with Tom's frame of mind. Suddenly she can understand why an agent might be justified in lying to another agent. And suddenly she can understand why an agent would consider breaking the rules — or pushing another agent to do so.

Which brings us to Diana's relationship with Marco Pacella, the man who most often bends the rules for her. Diana probably hasn't given a lot of thought to what's behind her attraction, but McKenzie obviously has. "He's this bright fantastic dude whose *mind* totally rings Diana's bell," McKenzie rhapsodizes. "They have similar likes and fascinations. And she has this trust in him, quite an intimate trust, which she doesn't seem to have in anyone else. Diana will defer to Tom in police matters *most* of the time. But I think with Marco she'd defer at *any* time, particularly in personal matters. She feels safe with him and respects him."

It takes a lot to generate that kind of response from Skouris. Like Tom Baldwin, she's a person used to doing things on her own. "She never really got on with her sister, because her sister chose the lazy options through life," McKenzie says, explaining Diana's mindset. "Diana worked her proverbial ass off to rise from where they grew up, with the alcoholic father and the sick mother who eventually died. Then she kind of stripped herself of what all the other people her age were doing — running around and partying. That stuff didn't happen for her."

But apparently Diana feels capable of such possibilities when she's around Marco, and despite the fact that the producers would split up the pair during the show's third season, McKenzie still feels they deserve a chance. "I want Diana to be with Marco. I still think that's the right way to go."

And what about season three's Ben (Brennan Elliott), future boyfriend of April Skouris, whom Maia has predicted is Diana's true Mister Right? "I'm hoping that he turns out to be some really *bad* person," confides McKenzie. But if it turns out that Marco isn't the one, the actress has another candidate at the top of her wish list of love interests for Diana Skouris: "Did I happen to mention Jon Favreau?" McKenzie asks innocently. "He's charismatic and funny and an unbelievable actor. I think it would take someone that remarkable to really shake Diana up!" ○

Richard Tyler

"Eventually a man's got to take a stand. I'm making mine right here."

Richard Tyler: Age thirty. African American. D.O.B.: 9/18/22. Disappeared: 5/11/51, while an Air Force pilot in the Korean War. Honors: Purple Heart, two Air Medals, Distinguished Flying Cross. In love with Lily Moore's grandmother, Lily Bonham, before he was abducted. Education: Bachelor of Science in Physical Education; Civilian Pilot Training Program graduate. — season two production notes

One has to imagine that Mahershalalhashbaz Ali's name drew at least a second glance when it showed up on the casting roster for *The 4400*. "Yeah, it looks a little scary at first," admits the man who plays Richard Tyler. It's a biblical name — actually the *longest* name in the Bible — referenced in the Book of Isaiah. The original Mahershalalhashbaz was one of the prophet Isaiah's sons. The current one, or at least the only one with a role in an ongoing television series, is a graduate of New York University's Tisch School of the Arts who holds a Masters degree in acting. Ali had grown up feeling confident that he had a totally unique first name. But then a friend of his happened to attend a conference in Las Vegas, "And he told me he ran into a guy who had it on his name tag," notes the actor. "I was disappointed at the time. I got a little territorial!"

Ali's audition for *The 4400* certainly received more than a second glance from the producers, who'd been thinking in a different direction for Richard Tyler. To a person, they all had the same reaction — that they'd somehow lucked into finding a guy who truly seems to have stepped out of the 1950s.

Ali smiles when he hears the comment. "While I was at school, the program I was in put a lot of emphasis on 'transformation'," he relates. "Transformational acting. Something about that clicked for me. It made sense. From the time that I was a little kid and playing at being someone, I always wanted to go as deep as I could and be that person for a moment in time. So as far as seeming to them like I was someone from the fifties, I like to think that if they'd asked me to play someone from 1993, they'd have said, 'You know, he really seemed like he stepped out of 1993.'

"I could tell that it was a good audition," he adds. "When I walked out I thought, 'That was in the pocket.' But I had to come back five or six more times because they were searching for the woman to play Lily. So I had to keep running the lines over and over again, and you know, once you've done a scene more than a couple of times, it can lose its life a little bit. But I felt like I couldn't slack back — I really had to be on. I was glad that it took so long though, because they eventually found Laura [Allen] and we just clicked in a certain way. We'd run into each other a few times in

New York so we kind of knew each other. But when we actually started working together, the chemistry felt right."

"Ali is phenomenal to work with," says Laura Allen with a broad smile. "He's such a gentleman. And he's so kind. He seems to have this innocence. You know what I think? I think that he was very close to his grandparents and he absorbed a lot of their manners and their values."

Ali does use recollections of his family to prepare himself for a scene. "I have some images of what my parents look like," he says. "And I've thought about the kinds of things that Richard's father and mother would have said to him, just to root him into something. The writers never dealt with Richard's parents on the show, and I felt that was a big hole, that Richard didn't have any roots. He wasn't connected. He never dealt with his family." When Richard was returned after a fifty-year absence, Ali goes on, it made sense that he would miss the original Lily, and that was covered in the story. "But I do think there could have been a stronger balance if they'd also shown that he really missed his family: his mom and dad and brother and sister," Ali confesses.

The relationship between Richard and the beautiful Lily Moore, granddaughter of Tyler's original lover Lily Bonham, was one of the emotional touchstones that helped to sell the series. The fact that they were a mixed race couple didn't receive much discussion internally, although it rose as a peripheral plot point when Richard initially interpreted the odd looks that he and Lily received as a couple as the result of racial prejudice. "In truth, the couple were being stared at because they were 4400s," says Maira Suro. "That's the present day stigma. Richard learns that he's living in a world that still can view him with unkind eyes, but for a different reason."

"The fact that he happens to be black and she happens to be white and they're together isn't really ever mentioned on the show," says Ali. "I found that really interesting."

"We didn't feel the need to hang a big neon sign over it," explains Scott Peters. "It's just the way the world is. And if you don't like that, too bad."

But if it wasn't mentioned by any of the characters on the show, it was mentioned by a small percentage of the viewers. "There was a bit of internet reaction,

saying 'This is not a healthy relationship to show on TV,'" comments Robert Hewitt Wolfe. "We were surprised by that, actually. Maybe there hasn't been as much progress in some areas as we thought when we developed the characters."

But the negative comments were balanced out by positive personal encounters. "I had a lot of people come up to me and say, 'You and Lily are like me and my husband,'" Ali reflects. "They'd tell me what they'd gone through themselves and then say, 'I'm just so glad you're on TV.' Because when you think about it, how many interracial relationships have you seen on TV over the years?"

The nagging question of whether or not Isabelle is actually Richard's child also doesn't seem to matter plot-wise, and the writers opted not to definitively address the issue. Certainly they provided viewers with that impression in the final episode of season one, when they revealed that the baby carried the genetic trait for sickle cell anemia, a disease that primarily affects people of African descent. For Richard, the revelation helps to back up a "divine alignment" of facts, as Ali puts it. "Because Lily looks exactly like her grandmother, Richard has already accepted the baby *could* be his," he says, although he can't define the circumstances of what might have transpired in order for the child to be conceived. "He definitely began to believe it at a certain point, and gave himself over to the belief." Noting that Richard committed to the idea that they would be together for the long haul in the scene where Lily told him she was apartment-hunting for the three of them (in 'The New and Improved Carl Morrissey'), Ali says, "Being with her gave him a sense of family. And it wasn't because they were 4400s." ○

"I know what the baby is thinking."

Lily Moore Tyler: Age twenty-eight. D.O.B.: 8/4/66. Disappeared: 5/26/93. Daughter Heidi was six months old when Lily disappeared. Husband Brian Moore married Carol while Lily was gone and they have a young son together. Lily was pregnant upon her return, possibly impregnated by Richard (unbeknownst to either of them) while they were abducted. Lily's parents were divorced when she was fourteen. Grandmother was Lily Bonham, of St Louis (died before Lily was born). Education: two years in community college. — season two production notes

"When I first read the 'Pilot' script, it didn't occur to me that Richard would be an African American," muses Laura Allen. "It didn't feel like a social commentary — the characters seemed to transcend that. Because it was a sci-fi piece and because the central premise is rooted in this really strange circumstance, it seemed to me that the script was more about finding human understanding.

"I was very moved by the idea of playing a mother whose child has grown up without her. And from a professional point of view, it felt good to be at the center of a show. Especially early on, I felt that Lily and Richard were at its heart. They both regretted losing the lives they'd had before, but they were looking forward and moving past that."

Allen finds it easy to identify with Lily on multiple levels. "I grew up in Seattle, and I was there during the same years that Lily supposedly was," she explains. "I left there in 1992 to go to college in Boston, close to the same time that Lily was abducted. So it was no trouble for me to personalize the location and the era Lily experienced. And after you do a show for a while, the writers find ways of getting into the actor's way of thinking. They start to learn you and they learn your voice and how you say things."

Like several of her fellow cast members, Allen has created a backstory for her character. "I feel that she met Brian when she was really young," she says. "He was in law school and taking his exams. And because Lily seems to operate so much from the heart, I assume she didn't make her professional life her priority. Her life was about being a wife and later a mother and that's it. I imagine they were living very modestly."

Lily's return, as Allen envisions it, "was almost like a classical mythological homecoming. She's been on this odyssey and then she came home expecting to be celebrated and brought back into the fold. When she isn't, she loses all hope of having a home. She goes to the old place and meets two girls at the door, and she doesn't even know which girl is hers. It's her own daughter, her own doorstep... and

her own *husband*, who's suddenly eleven years older than she remembers him. It's devastating for her. And then on top of that, she finds out she's pregnant. She does the calculations and remembers that before she disappeared, Brian had been taking exams, so they hadn't been intimate — which means he couldn't have been involved. So the fact that she's pregnant just doesn't seem possible.

"Once she and Richard connect, she makes her home in *him*. And when the possibility comes up that he might be the father of her baby, it's the only thing she can grab on to, so I think that's what she chooses to believe."

As the series' second season opened, Lily and Richard suddenly found themselves thrown into a kind of "Bonnie and Clyde" scenario, living life on the run. "We felt like we were shooting our own independent movie," she recalls, "with everybody else back at NTAC or the 4400 Center. We started filming in February in Canada, running through the woods with the baby. We were lucky that the rain didn't stop us from shooting very often, but it *was* cold. We were shooting in gas stations and cabins and traipsing up and down hills, and there were moments when it felt like some kind of eerie Hitchcock film."

Lily appeared in ten of the second season's thirteen episodes, reports Allen, "and the ones that I was in seemed pretty Lily-intensive to me, so I never felt there was a lack of storyline for her." The actress also covered a lot of emotional territory as the character evolved. "Lily began to shift her priorities to Isabelle, and to the things she felt a mother needs to do to make ends meet and feed and protect the baby. She overrides Richard's old-fashioned morals by choosing to steal — that's the first sign that there's a shift between them. Then they get to the town where Richard's friend

lives, and he wants to stay there. The emotional distance between them grows and she finds she can't communicate with him, which pushes her deeper into her relationship with Isabelle."

Which is perhaps why Lily is so surprised when the baby eventually cuts off communication with her and switches to "talking" to dad as they settle in at the 4400 Center. According to the writers, Lily's only 4400 ability had been the fact that she could communicate on an emotional level with her child. And now, that was suddenly taken away from her.

"If Laura had remained on the series, I suspect we would have eventually given her something else," observes Craig Sweeny.

But the best laid plans don't always happen. Although the writers were prepared to carry Lily's storyline into the series' third season, it was not to be. "A few months after we'd finished season two, I decided not to go back," Allen explains. The decision was, as Michael Corleone would say, "just business", and the parting was cordial for all concerned. In fact, Allen greatly enjoyed watching her "replacement" in 'The New World', the opening episode of season three.

"I was just *thrilled* when I heard that Tippi Hedren was going to play the older Lily," Allen enthuses. "What an honor! I love *The Birds*, and I love her, so it was so flattering to me to know that she'd seen the show and watched my work on it. It's hard to let a character that you've been developing for two years go, but I think she handled it with such grace that I was glad to see her carry on the tradition."

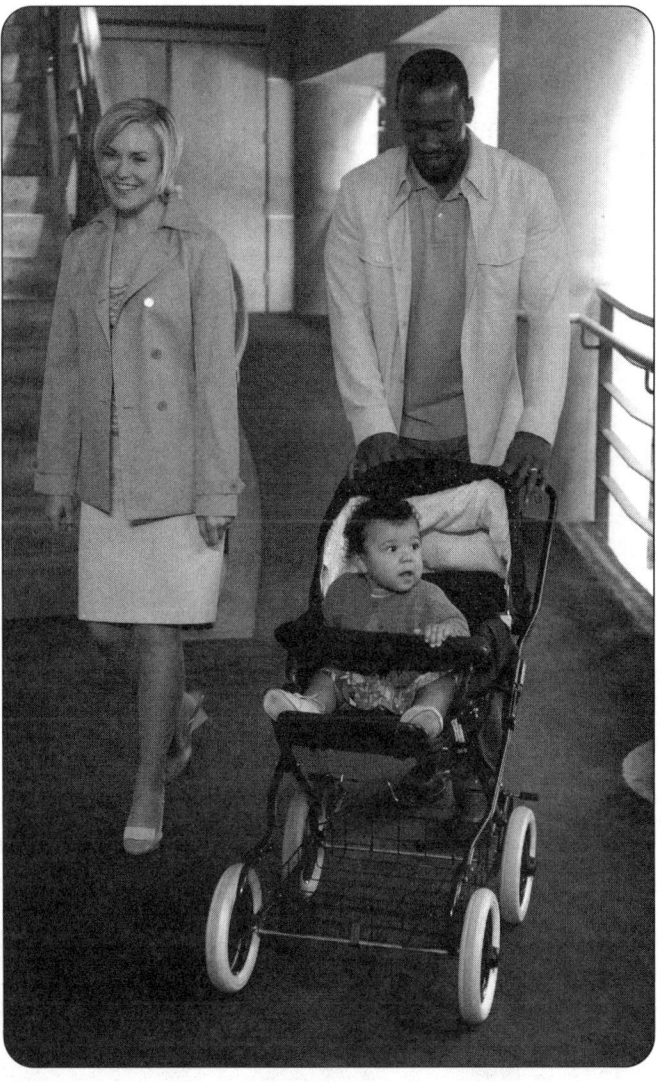

And who knows what the future holds? Allen notes that she's spoken with the producers and co-star Mahershalalhashbaz Ali about possible storylines that could bring the old Lily — Lily Bonham, that is — into the show somewhere down the road, possibly in flashbacks.

After all, in a show like *The 4400*, the possibilities are endless — and dead doesn't always mean dead. O

Shawn Farrell

"A week ago I was just some guy trying to beat the last level of *Doom*. I wasn't the Pope then and I'm not the Pope now."

Shawn Farrell: Age eighteen. D.O.B.: 12/12/83. Disappeared: 4/22/01 from Highland Beach, WA. Mother: Susan Kincaid (father's name unestablished). Brother: Danny Farrell. Mother is sister to Tom Baldwin. Shawn's cousin Kyle Baldwin was with him on the night he was abducted. Returned to high school as a junior, but left school and his family to work with Jordan Collier. Took over the 4400 Center when Collier was killed. — season two production notes

"We weren't sure what we wanted from the character of Shawn initially," states Ira Behr. "He was only seventeen. So what kind of 'life interrupted' could we give him? He wouldn't have an ex-wife or kids. We already had a parental figure with Tom and we were going to do that with Diana too. So it became the brother thing. I'm always interested in that whole male bonding thing and there was something interesting about the idea of these two, a younger brother who once looked up to an older brother and then the older brother comes back and suddenly he's no longer 'older' — he's the same age. And the younger brother's carved out a place for himself but the other brother seems to be taking away what this kid feels he's earned — a relationship with this girl."

If there was a triangle between Shawn, his brother Danny and Danny's girlfriend Nikki, there also was one between Shawn, Danny and their cousin Kyle Baldwin. Of the three, Shawn would experience the most growth as a character. (While Kyle's Job-like travails as a pawn of the future people keep bouncing him around emotionally, they don't offer him much opportunity to grow.) But while the producers trusted that Patrick

Flueger could play the first part of the arc, they couldn't be sure if he'd be able to stretch into the more mature character that becomes head of the 4400 Center. "Patrick had auditioned as the t-shirt-wearing slacker, the angst-ridden kid," explains Ira Behr. "We knew he could handle that. But he really stepped up after we killed off Jordan. He did a *great* job. Good actors make you rethink the characters they play, and I really, really, really respect what Patrick did in the second half of the second season."

Yves Simoneau, director of the 'Pilot', probably could have predicted that reaction. "Patrick was a real asset from early on," he says. "We discovered that very quickly. He has a real presence, an ease to himself that is very rare. He's very comfortable, and he's not afraid of going to places where it's a little more complicated emotionally. He actually looks forward to that kind of thing. He's not just a pretty boy."

"Directing him is great — it's really fun to watch him," confirms Scott Peters. "He comes in and has a direction that sometimes is dead on and sometimes isn't, like a lot of actors. But he's so open to moving in a direction that unlocks his potential. That's what I love about Patrick. If you give him another take, he'll always invent something different. He's never going to do the same thing over and over again."

That's appropriate for the actor who portrays the 4400 with the most powerful gift. Flueger would need to be able to convey the double-edged nature of Shawn's ability. "Initially, his ability was just to heal," Peters says. "But then we felt that it would be beneficial to the story mix if he could also reverse that ability and take *away* life as well. That became a very powerful aspect of what Shawn could do, and a dangerous one too, because if you overuse it in stories, you may as well put a cape on him and turn him into a superhero."

By all accounts, Flueger is nearly as complex as Shawn, and his co-workers seem to enjoy the yin and yang of his nature — particularly his more mischievous side.

"Patrick is the most social guy in the cast," chuckles Laura Allen. "He loves to go out and play and have fun. Kind of like a little kid. I felt very sisterly towards him."

"At one point, he wanted to buzz-cut his hair, something that would really change his character's look, and we had to say, 'Absolutely not!'" recalls Peters with a laugh. "He said,

'Why not?' so we told him, 'We paid for the hottie of the show and you're gonna be the hottie of the show.' Patrick understood, but I suspect that the minute he finishes with Shawn for the season, he does things with his appearance that get him away from the character."

"He has this duality," observes Joel Gretsch. "He's so smart and so worldly and he really has a handle on just about everything. And then there's this part of him — this twenty-year-old kid that you just want to send to his room and say, 'Don't come out of there!' He's so mature that sometimes you forget how young he is. He's perfect for the role because Shawn's like that too. He's trying to do his best for the Center, but there's still this mischievous kid inside who's likely to do some stuff that isn't so mature." Gretsch admits to having a soft spot for both Flueger and Chad Faust. "In many ways I feel like they're my boys. And I have a protective feeling about them, particularly Patrick. He grew up in a small town — Red Wing, Minnesota — and I'm from Minnesota too. He's an extremely talented guy."

Flueger credits the people who put the words on paper for the success of his portrayal. "The writers on this show are just phenomenal," he says. "It's a science fiction show but it's really about the people and the relationships. And that comes through in spades. It's very easy to play Shawn. Not because I'm a lot like him, but because it's kind of all there on the page. He's an absolutely wonderful character to play and I couldn't be happier." ○

Kyle Baldwin

> "I'm blacking out, losing chunks of time. It's like they did something to my wiring... They left me messed up inside."

Kyle Baldwin: Age twenty-one. D.O.B.: 8/9/84. On Highland Beach, WA with his cousin Shawn Farrell 4/22/01. He was supposed to be abducted but Shawn interfered and was taken instead. Kyle lapsed into a three-year-long coma that night, ultimately awakened by Shawn after Shawn's return. Kyle's body was still inhabited by a person from the future until his return to Highland Beach (in 'White Light'), at which point he appeared to become his former self. — season two production notes

It's hard for regular viewers of *The 4400* not to get the impression that Kyle Baldwin is the Job of the series. He seems to get dumped on by higher powers more often than any other character in the series. First he spends three years in a vegetative state and misses out not only on the opportunity to become a channel for the "future people", but also on his senior year of high school. Then his body is inhabited by one of those future people. And then, after *that* person seems to check out, yet *another* future person takes over, using Kyle's body to kill Jordan Collier, resulting in prison time for Kyle until Collier resurfaces months later...

Ira Behr shrugs. "On this show, *everyone* gets messed with a lot," he says with a smile. "But there's no reason to have this kid unless you're messing with him. You can't do *Father Knows Best* on *The 4400*. Kyle's role is to make things difficult for Tom — and for himself. But the kid keeps you on his side for the most part. There's an innocence in him, more a 'sinned against' than 'sinning' aspect to him that I think is likeable."

It's enough to make an actor... confused. "Honestly, I'm still not sure if I actually know who Kyle Baldwin is," sighs Chad Faust. "This character is so different from anyone I've ever played. Usually I have a clear idea of who somebody is and what they want, but even in the most recent episodes I've still been riding on this concept that this is a guy who doesn't know what he's doing here and what his purpose is in life. But it's the greatest acting job ever. There are so many different versions of Kyle. I tried to count them once and I think I came up with six different versions that I'd gotten to play."

That Faust got to play so many facets of a character that everyone on the set had originally thought of as simply "the coma kid" was not originally in the cards. "Kyle was not supposed to be in that many episodes," says Scott Peters. "But because his story arc kept intersecting with the other characters, he became much more important. And once we started shooting the episodes, we saw that the pain that

Joel brought to his performance as Tom, and what Chad brought to his portrayal of Kyle, was absolute gold."

"Chad is a terrific actor," says Yves Simoneau. "I knew he wasn't going to be able to show that in the 'Pilot' episode I directed, but everybody was looking at the future and they all had the end in mind. They knew where they'd want him to be later on, and I can tell you that we all chose him for his acting qualities." He pauses and smiles. "On the other hand, he does have a very interesting look, even when he's resting. Just the way his face is cut makes it interesting to film." So even Simoneau got exactly what he wanted from Faust!

The belief that Faust could carry off his scenes beyond the coma phase was extremely important to the producers. "We knew that as the show progressed, Kyle would start interacting with Tom," relates Peters. "Early on, our impression of Tom is that he's the best father in the world. He's at Kyle's bedside every minute, trying to do everything he can to figure out how he got there. But after Kyle comes around, some things begin to come to light, like maybe Tom *isn't* the greatest father in the world, and maybe being at his son's bedside was his way of trying to make up for it. Good stories have conflict, and there were a lot of different aspects of the relationship that he'd have to play."

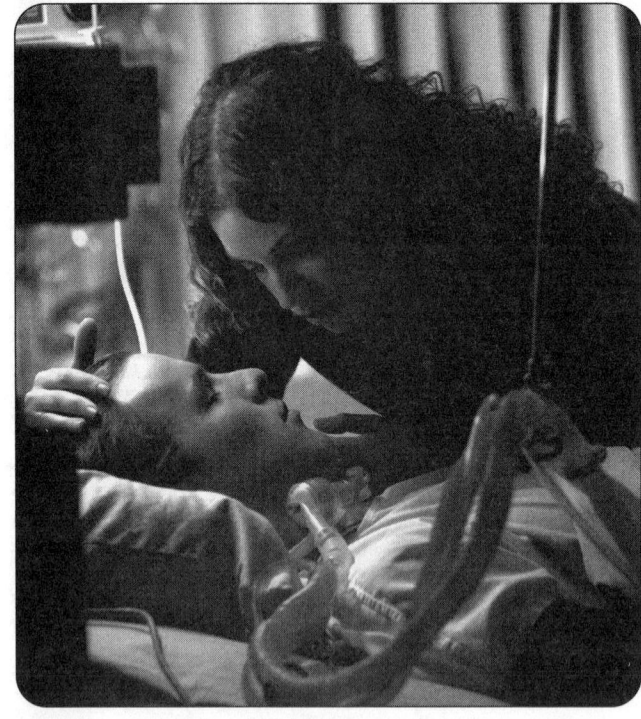

Peters was impressed with Faust's willingness to go the extra mile to get his portrayal right. "We were getting ready to shoot the first episode after Kyle wakes up," recalls Peters, "and I saw Chad in the morning and asked him what he'd done over the weekend. He said, 'I spent my weekend at a nursing home.' Then he explained that he'd hung out there observing how people who've been convalescing learn to walk again and eat again and talk again. I thought, 'Wow, a young actor who takes his role so seriously that he's sitting at a nursing home instead of partying.' I love Chad. I think he's a tremendous actor."

The second season of the series would bring Faust even greater challenges, as his character becomes the pawn of someone from the future who wants Jordan Collier dead. But for

all the pain, there is also gain, as Kyle finally gets a decent wardrobe... and the perks that accompany hot clothes. "In the first season I mostly wore hospital smocks," Faust laughs. "And then when Kyle went home, he had on sweat pants — that kind of thing. I thought, 'Man, I'll never get laid — all because of Kyle.' But in the second season, they started dressing me in really great clothes, the kind of stuff *I'd* wear if I had a stylist shopping for me." The result? Kyle had onscreen flirtations with three different women over the course of the season — and at least one definite score. If Faust didn't have similar success, he can't blame the threads.

The reason for the change was the visual balancing act that the producers were trying to suggest between Kyle and Shawn. "They decided to give me a hip grungy look, to set me apart from Patrick's character," says Faust. "In the first season, Shawn was the grungy one, but after he took over the Center, they put him in more conservative business-type wear. They wanted to keep us at polar opposites."

Faust has taken the extrapolation even farther. "I always see Shawn and Kyle as being two brothers on the opposite sides of a civil war," he explains. "In the first episode of season two ['Wake-Up Call'], they get together and at first they're happy to see each other, but one's fighting for the North and one for the South and..." His voice trails off and he chuckles. "And then in the last episode of season two ['Mommy's Bosses'], when he takes that 'being' out of me, it's clear we're still on different sides, but at least we can help each other out." ○

Maia Rutledge Skouris

"I don't want to know things before they happen. I want to be normal, like I used to be."

Maia Rutledge Skouris: Age nine. D.O.B.: 2/28/38. Disappeared: 3/3/46 from Crescent City, CA. Parents: Ethan (1905-1981) and Mary Rutledge (1913-1990). Education prior to abduction: third grade. First 4400 taken. Initially placed with foster family the Griffiths. Formally adopted by Diana Skouris in June, 2005. — season two production notes

"The thing about children and acting ability is that when they have it, they have it perfectly," notes Yves Simoneau. "They may lose it later when they grow up, but when they have it, it's really a natural thing. They have it in their heart, in their bones, in their soul. And that's what Conchita has. She really nailed it."

As the man charged with directing the 'Pilot' for *The 4400*, Simoneau studied each of the newly cast actors very carefully, and tried to guide and nurture those qualities that he knew would become their defining traits as the series moved forward. Simoneau knew at once that Conchita Campbell would have no problems. "There was some light in her," he comments. "We knew there was something very special about her, and when I started shooting, I quickly realized that she could sustain — she could be the center of a scene. She was very flexible and her instincts were impeccable. I was curious to see what she would come up with if I let her approach something from her own point of view — and she was able to deliver there, too. She was a pro, a young little pro that seemed as if she'd been on a set forever."

Although veteran actor Peter Coyote shared only one scene with Campbell, he too sensed that there was something special in the then eight-year-old actor. "Children have a pretty fluid sense of reality because they haven't learned yet what's possible and what isn't," he states. "So when they commit to something in their imagination, they really commit. It's like working with a really experienced actor, where you find that you're sharing common imaginative space. And I didn't detect any 'seams' in Conchita's performance. There was nothing that hinted to me that she didn't believe in what she was saying or doing. You know, it's very, very hard to find an eight-year-old that's mature enough to handle all of the sitting around and waiting that's inherent in film-making without becoming a discipline problem."

The producers of *The 4400* were well aware of those difficulties. "We thought for sure that the character of Maia was going to be the downfall of the show," observes Scott Peters. "In fact, we were prepared to write the role down because we didn't think we were going to find someone who could pull off the role with the gravitas

that it required. Conchita was the third person we saw for Maia. The first two made us slap our hands to our foreheads and say, 'We've gotta start rewriting *now*.' Then we saw Conchita's tape and after her first take, there was silence in the room. But we waited to see the second take before we said anything, just in case it was a fluke. But the second take was brilliant. And we all looked at each other and said, 'If she can do this on a weekly basis, we've really got something.' For someone that young to have that much knowledge about how everything works, and to be able to slip into and out of that world, going from being this regular kid to this character who delivers those chilling one-liners — well, it's amazing."

But it's all child's play to Campbell, who explains her technique in a very matter-of-fact way. "All little kids are into gags and stuff, right?" she says. "Well, before I start the day, I think of what my scenes are and I think, 'Maia's gonna do this today.' And then when it's my turn, I do my scene and then if I have a break, I'll play, or maybe go to school. But as soon as I hear, 'Okay, we're gonna roll now,' I go back to it and do it."

And according to the people she works with, that's exactly the way it happens. "Absolutely true," comments Natasha Gregson Wagner. "She'll be laughing and playing and kidding around, being a little girl, and the minute the camera comes on, she's completely self-possessed."

"Conchita's full of energy and bouncing off the walls when she's not on camera," says Maira Suro. "But the minute the director says 'Action' — boom! — she's focused. At this point, going into season four, we've had our issues with some people arriving on the set unprepared, not knowing their lines, going in and out of character. But Conchita? Never. She's so on the money."

"I kind of think of her as someone like Jeff Combs [who plays Kevin Burkhoff]," Ira Behr relates wryly. "Jeff plays these *outrageous* characters, but given the fact that he's an actor, he's a fairly normal guy, someone I like to hang out with. And Conchita is a totally normal girl, but when she gets that inward thing going, with those *eyes* of hers..."

Campbell giggles at the mention of her eyes. "Yeah,

everyone always tells me, 'Oooh, I love your eyes.' I don't really think of Maia as scary. More like a creepy little girl. Kind of mysterious and creepy at the same time. Sometimes my friends and I have these staring contests, where you try to keep your eyes open. And I'll look at them with 'the creepy face' and sometimes it makes them blink on purpose just to make me stop 'cause they're getting too creeped out looking at me!"

"We've done some really nice scenes with Conchita, sad stuff where she misses her parents or when her foster parents return her," says Behr. "But other times we use her as 'witchy woman', where she comes out with this enigmatic spooky line and we see those eyes and then — 'Cut!'" He chuckles. "As the seasons have gone on, we've been able to do more stuff and get more colors with her."

Like many of her fellow actors, Campbell tries to use her own experiences to motivate her for a scene. When she has to deliver those witchy woman lines, she takes her time by inserting pauses at strategic points, "because whenever I've seen other scary shows, I find that *I* get creeped out when the people take their time," she says. "So I do that too." She thinks about sad things when she's supposed to cry, or maybe things like the bad dreams that made her run crying to her mother, Magdalena Campbell... when she was younger, of course. "That's basically how I prepare," she says. "I just go with my heart."

These days, as a more mature actor, Campbell prefers to read and watch DVDs in her trailer when she's not in a scene. "And my teacher showed me these books of Sudoku puzzles, and I like to play with them," she says. And especially welcome is the occasional set visit from Coco, her miniature dachshund. "She's so small, she can fit her head under my armpit!" Campbell giggles. "She's really cute." ○

Jordan Collier: Early forties. Disappeared: 4/10/2002. Hotel and casino owner/businessman. Six federal indictments vs his businesses over the years. 'Zapped' by Isabelle, this experience caused the internal shift that led to his founding the 4400 Center and writing his manifesto, 4400 and Counting. Murdered by Kyle Baldwin's alter-ego. — season two production notes

> "I've been given a second chance to do something with my life besides make money"

"Some things are difficult for me to play," admits Billy Campbell. "Powerful, sexy, self-confident people are hard because — I don't know — I guess I feel silly playing them."

Can this possibly be the man who embodies Jordan Collier? It can — and, in fact, it's part of the underlying reason for the 'beard incident' that occurred on Campbell's very first day of shooting *The 4400* (for the episode 'Becoming'). "I always feel more confident when I have a beard," he says, "less self-conscious than when I'm clean-shaved. So I was determined to keep my beard if I was going to play Jordan Collier. I told the producers that I couldn't cut it off because I might need it for a role, but... that wasn't entirely true."

Not many actors would roll the dice on losing such a showy part. But Campbell did — twice, in fact. He also had to let his potential employers know that he wouldn't be available for a long-term assignment. "I already had this trip planned, so I told them right away: 'I'll do your TV series, but I'm sailing around the world for a year.'"

"He was very upfront about it," says Scott Peters. But the producers knew that he was the right actor, and that led them to devise Collier's assassination — as well as his ultimate resurrection. "The last thing I told Billy before he left was, 'Don't die on your trip!'" Peters laughs.

Campbell's voyage was also the inspiration for Collier's unofficial ability. "I'd always wondered if I had one, and I kept asking the producers about it," Campbell says. "And then one day Scotty [Peters] came to me and he was so excited that he could barely contain himself. 'Your ability is *immortality*!' And I was like, 'Really?'"

Is Collier a good guy or a bad guy? "I have no idea," Campbell reveals. "The producers refuse to tell me. I get to find out on a weekly basis, as the scripts come down."

"I think there's a bit of an internal struggle going on within Jordan from the very beginning," says Ira Behr. "Was he there to be a resource for the 4400 or to control it? Would he answer to the better angels or the darker angels of his nature?"

After Isabelle zapped him, Collier's struggle seemed to crystallize. "Once he realized how powerful Isabelle was, he glommed on to her right away," notes Behr. "There was a reason for this baby's existence and he wanted to know what it was. It's like the ring that Gollum covets. The baby became Jordan's 'precious'."

But Isabelle is just the personification of what's most important to Collier. "Power," states Behr. "Power that most people never even dream of. He thinks of controlling the future, controlling the world — or maybe saving the world, but only if he's the one to do it. It has nothing to do with money. He's *way* beyond money."

Dennis Ryland: Head of the Northwest NTAC office at the time of the 4400's return. Old friend and colleague of Tom Baldwin. — season two production notes

> **"I haven't changed. I have a tough job. I'm doing my best."**

"When we developed Ryland, we saw him as a guy who was in a situation that was over his head," explains Robert Hewitt Wolfe. "A lot of what went into him was informed by 9/11. Dennis Ryland represented an old-school guy in a world that no longer made old-school sense. That's what a lot of guys in the FBI faced after 9/11. Their reality, the things they knew how to do, changed on that day. That was the analogy for us: what does someone who was trained to respond in a specific way to a crisis do when the universe suddenly changes in a fundamental way?"

"Normally I'm not too interested in science fiction," admits Ryland's alter ego, Peter Coyote, "but the 'Pilot' was a really good script and my part was interesting. I realized that it was a misnomer to dismiss *The 4400* as generic science fiction. It's not. The best science fiction works as a morality play — a place to deal with *ideas*, like the huge global event in the 'Pilot' that becomes the catalyst for the whole series."

"In the original pitch, Ryland was Tom and Diana's boss," Scott Peters explains. "He was the guy that was going to send them on their assignments and be the voice of authority. The fact that he evolved, and turned in the way he did, kind of happened as we were writing him. And Peter adapted as you'd hope an actor would. No one thinks of himself as bad; he thinks he's doing the right thing. Ryland believes that these people are bad for us and that he's protecting the world. In his mind, he's a hero."

Coyote, who's possibly as well known for championing political and environmental causes as he is for acting, enjoys the recurring role. "What could be more fun than to be given a platform to interpret your feelings about the politics of our current administration through your character?" he says with a smile.

"Although in fairness to Ryland, I always felt that he initially had a very strong argument for what he did. But as time went on, he became more reprehensible and began crossing the line, and in doing so, he's gotten farther off the mainstream, and deeper into his own mental fantasy."

Nina Jarvis: New head of the Northwest NTAC office as of June 2005. Successor to Dennis Ryland. — season two production notes

> "I need results. We have a high-priced collection of sheepskin in the basement that tells me you're the best way to get them."

Actor Samantha Ferris's strong sense of self-confidence came in handy when Peter Coyote left *The 4400* and the casting call went out for the new head of NTAC's Northwest division. "Ryland's a pretty ominous character," points out the Vancouver native. "And they felt they needed a very specific successor to fill his shoes: a woman who had some balls, but was capable of caring about her staff. And I happen to be that type. I have a very strong voice and I carry a lot of power with me. And ultimately, I was the one who personified what they were looking for."

Ferris appreciated the producers' decision to make Ryland's replacement a woman; in the twenty-first century it's not always men in charge, she states. "Being

a woman, Nina had to work twice as hard to get where she is. So I play her as if I'm a heavy duty workaholic," she says. "It's all-consuming for Nina, so she doesn't go home and laugh it up."

The producers haven't, as yet, given Nina a home life. "That separates her from the rest of the characters," she notes. "You get to see their emotional sides, what makes them tick. But as Nina, I'm not really allowed to show my emotions. I have to keep my act together and stay constant. If I were allowed to play vulnerable, the NTAC office would fall apart. So I'm always the bitch with pearls — the tough voice that just happens to be a woman."

Despite the lack of backstory, Ferris has some ideas about Jarvis. "When I first came in, the props guy handed me a wedding ring. I said, 'Really? I'm married?' I don't know if Nina's husband is dead or what. But personally I think she's got some dark stories inside. There's some pain there, and she may be a bit of a boozer. Nina's definitely not just a case of what you see is what you get."

Marco Pacella: Theory room tech and friend of Diana's. He wrote the paper that got Tom reassigned to active duty. — season two production notes

> "I just opened a 401K. Yeah, I'm pretty sure the government stops matching donations once you commit treason."

Richard Kahan brought a box of corn pops to his audition. "There were many, many people trying out, and I just wanted to bring the right idea to the table," he says with a grin. "So there I was, snacking on the corn pops while I was interacting with the other characters in the scene. In my mind, that's part of who Marco is. He's a multi-tasker. He's always got so much stuff on his plate that he's just *go, go, go*! Marco doesn't have time to sit down and eat scrambled eggs."

It was a great intuitive choice. "I immediately glommed onto Richard's performance in his audition tape," says Ira Behr. "He came on like Quentin Tarantino, so passionate about some subject matter that he's *lecturing* you, and there's no room for argument — which doesn't matter because he's giving a performance you *want* to listen to. Richard had that same quality. He came off like he was a hell of a lot smarter than you, and that he could make connections you could never see, but you'd be a fool not to listen to him."

"That's my favorite thing about Marco," Kahan admits. "He's constantly coming

up with the big discovery. And that makes Tom and Diana want to turn to him more, because they know they can always count on Marco. I refer to him as the 'quirky sidekick'."

Jacqueline McKenzie appreciates Marco as much as Diana. "He's not some enter-stage-right spunky dude with a six pack of abs," she says. "Oh, that would be boring, boring!"

Diana's personal relationship with Marco grew during season two, culminating with a romantic kiss in 'Mommy's Bosses'. "On one level, Marco and Diana is a strange pairing," Kahan admits, "but on another it really makes sense. They're two peas in the same pod, because of their backgrounds. So it was fun for me to play the guy who gets the girl — or at least pursues her, even if they did cut a lot of our scenes together!"

"That was our fault," admits Behr. "The scenes were always being cut for time. We eventually had to break them up and I actually felt bad for Marco." However, Behr admits that he's already thinking of ways to make it up to him in a coming season.

Danny Farrell: Age eighteen. Mother: Susan Kincaid (father's name unestablished). Brother: Shawn Farrell. Mother is sister to Tom Baldwin. Was dating Nikki Hudson until she broke up with him to begin seeing Shawn. — season two production notes

> **"If you expect me to apologize and kiss your robe, you're wasting your time."**

Prior to being cast in *The 4400*, Kaj-Erik Eriksen was best known to television audiences from his recurring role on *The Commish*. "I've been working since I was about six years old," Eriksen says matter-of-factly. "I'm originally from Vancouver, so I've been lucky enough to keep getting roles on the shows that film here. When I got the script for *The 4400* 'Pilot', I read for the role of Shawn and also for Kyle. And about a week after I sent in my tape, I got a call saying, 'You're booked as Danny.' And I thought, 'Danny?'"

"Kaj is a really good actor," comments Ira Behr. "And he had a really good reel of clips. But we hired him before we knew that we were going to cast Patrick Flueger as his brother — and, well, they look pretty different when they stand next to each other!"

The difference between his height and Flueger's didn't phase Eriksen, and provided a rare touch of visual humor to the scene where Danny protects his brother from being whaled on by Brad. "Shawn's so much bigger than I am, but here's scrappy little Danny stepping in for him. We had a good laugh over that."

Eriksen hasn't really developed a backstory for his character. "When I get a script I tend to insert my own life experience into it, and think how I might react in a similar situation," he says. That certainly fired his response when Danny learned that Nikki and Shawn had slept together. "Danny never thought that he might be Nikki's second choice," says Eriksen. "He really likes her and thinks she likes him, which is what motivates the big fight between the brothers."

Nikki Hudson: Age eighteen. Next-door neighbor to the Farrell family. Danny's girlfriend until Shawn's return. — season two production notes

> **"That was you - you fixed him, just like you fixed my hand."**

There was a lot of discussion, in the offices and on the internet, about Nikki sleeping with Shawn," recalls Ira Behr. "But to me it was okay. There was already a pre-existing relationship in her head. It was like that thing you wanted more than anything when you were a kid — 'He's the coolest guy, but I'm too young so there's no way.' And maybe she was with Danny because of that. But then Shawn comes back, and through the miracle of television, she's now old enough to be with him! So she's got to be thinking, 'He's so lost and he needs someone — I can help him.' The lovemaking came out of character, which is where all motivation has to stem from."

That's pretty much the same way that Brooke Nevin sees it — although she feels Nikki had genuine affection for Danny. "I kind of imagine that being neighborhood kids, Nikki was close to both brothers," she muses. "And sometimes when a tragedy happens it draws two people closer. Danny was Nikki's age, so it's natural Shawn's disappearance would bring them together. I think there was a real tenderness between them."

Even after Shawn returns, it's not like the two of them immediately jump into bed, she notes. "Patrick and I talked a lot about how we wanted that relationship to develop. We didn't want it to seem as if the relationship was forced. We really wanted to convey the spiritual connection between them."

Although Nevin was a regular during the first season, she has appeared only intermittently on the series since then. In the alternate universe that Alana creates for Tom Baldwin in 'Life Interrupted', she winds up married to Danny, which in her mind proves her point about her and the younger Farrell. "We're the same people, no matter what," observes the quintessential girl next door. "It just depends on what path we take in life."

Matthew Ross: Lobbyist in the Collier organization who relocated to the Center in order to advise Shawn Farrell after Jordan Collier's death.

> "The Center is the new Lourdes. Nobody's going to be calling us a cult anymore."

"Actually, I initially thought that they wanted me to *be* Billy Campbell," Garrett Dillahunt says. "Or rather, that they wanted me to fill in as Jordan Collier while Billy was taking that big cruise." He chuckles over the misunderstanding. "When I realized that they meant that they wanted my character to *replace* Jordan's character… that was a little embarrassing."

Knowing that Campbell was a hard act to follow, the writers searched for a way to differentiate Ross's character from Collier's, and in the process they picked up on an interesting resemblance to a former director of the Christian Coalition and political activist for the Republican Party. "Suddenly we had a handle on Matthew," says Fred Rappaport. "He was the second coming of Ralph Reed."

"Matthew's definitely a hand shaker who knows how to move someone over to his special interests," Dillahunt says. "During my first year on the show, I thought Matthew had the best interests of the Center in mind. But it's kind of hard to get a fix on a character when you don't know what's going to happen next for him. By my second year, I guess the evil side of the future got a hold of me and began influencing me, using my skills at manipulation for their own ends."

The producers didn't explain too much about Ross's motivation to Dillahunt and they deliberately didn't explain it to the audience at all. "I like there to be mystery," Behr says emphatically. "We started out the series by giving away the farm. But I *like* there to be things that the audience isn't sure of. You can't spoon feed people — as much as they might want it."

Alana Mareva: Age thirty-three. D.O.B.: 10/17/69. Disappeared: 9/5/01. Husband and son killed in a car accident prior to her abduction. Returned with the ability to create alternate realities out of people's memories.

> **"None of this is real to me either."**

"I *wanted* Karina on the show," Ira Behr states emphatically. "I *wanted* her character in the show. I *wanted* Tom to have that strange relationship." When Behr met Karina Lombard on *Dr. Vegas* during the hiatus between seasons one and two of *The 4400*, something clicked. He realized that the Tahitian-born actor, best known to US audiences for her appearances on Showtime's *The L Word*, was the embodiment of Alana Mareva, the exotic woman sent by the future people to save Tom Baldwin's soul. "I saw them together immediately. I knew the chemistry would be there," Behr says. "The whole Fred Astaire/Ginger Rogers thing, with a twist. Fred gave Ginger class; Ginger gave Fred sex appeal. Tom is such a white bread kind of

guy, she would give him mystery; he would give her accessibility. It became an obsession to me."

Lombard was quite amenable to working with Behr on a second series. "When I did *Dr. Vegas*, I thought his writing was so great," she says. "And I could feel that same quality in this show. What you say has more meaning than just what the words say. I love that. Things are not always what they seem."

Alana is an enigma even to the woman who plays her. "There's definitely a part of her that is not *hers*, that belongs somewhere else," Lombard muses. "It may be part of a mission, or an agenda that is implanted in her. So I feel there is a constant conflict between the person who is aware and something within her that is a mystery even to her. Or maybe not! But that's how I play her."

Lombard loves Alana's 4400 ability. "Wouldn't you like it?" she teases. "If you're sad or in a bad place, you could escape. It's interesting because I have this strong belief that we're one hundred percent responsible for our lives — you create your own life. So this ability makes total sense to me, as a person and as an actor."

Kevin Burkhoff: Brilliant scientist, institutionalized at Abendson Hospital for six years, until the sound waves from Tess Doerner's tower healed him. Before his illness, he was a neuroscientist working to awaken dormant neural pathways. — season two production notes

> "I showed you mine. You show me yours."

"I wouldn't be in this series at all if it wasn't for the brilliant Ira Steven Behr," states Jeffrey Combs. After all, Combs' character initially had almost no dialogue and played only a peripheral role in the action. But Combs knew from experience that even the smallest role offered up by Behr could be quite rewarding, and everything turned out exactly as both men had envisioned.

"Everybody adored Jeff in 'Wake-Up Call', Behr says. "The folks at USA were a little unsure at first, because this is supposed to be a serious show, and Jeff brings..." Behr pauses. It's hard to define Combs' unique qualities, although there's always a touch of the quirky and darkly humorous in his performances. And those were exactly the characteristics Behr sought. "But what matters to me more than that," he adds, "is when I start hearing back from the set, 'This guy is *great!*' I just eat that stuff up."

"I love Jeff Combs," endorses Jacqueline McKenzie.

"I cannot wait to do a scene with him. He's such an inventive joy to work with. He brings so much to the table."

"It's hard not to love Jeff," confirms Joel Gretsch. "He's an adult with a kid's mind."

"He can play everything, from the quirky stuff with the sunflower seeds, to the vulnerability and the torment that we dealt him later on in the show," notes Behr.

"I played Kevin as very shut down and non-communicative," Combs says. "But I think that he knew instinctively what was going on. It's as if he had blown a fuse, and there was no juice going to the mainframe. Or maybe it was a choice," Combs adds with a shrug. "Maybe that was Kevin's version of forty days and forty nights in the desert."

Now, about those sunflower seeds — "You tell me," chuckles Combs. "That was in the script. It wasn't like I asked the prop guy for them. I suspect that the writers gave them to me to use as a device that would demonstrate some of Kevin's more unique social qualities!"

Brian Moore: Lily's former husband. He remarried (Carol) while Lily was gone. Father of Lily's daughter Heidi, he also has a son with Carol. — season two production notes

> **"It's been eleven years. I couldn't wait forever."**

It's not easy being Brian, ex-husband to Lily. "You loved this woman," Andrew Airlie says, putting himself in the mindset of the character he plays. "There were no issues when she left. It wasn't a matter of you two not getting along. You wanted her, you started a family with her. And now she's back in your life…"

…And you file a restraining order against her.

Airlie smiles ruefully. "I remember Scott Peters coming up to me one day and saying, 'Boy, did we ever get an emphatic response to your character. People really hate your guy.'" Particularly after Brian flashed that restraining order at Lily. "Well, that's hardly the nicest of gestures, is it?" he adds.

Director Yves Simoneau's words helped temper Airlie's performance in the 'Pilot'. "He impressed upon me that, yes, Brian was closing the door, but that I should find the humanity in the guy closing the door. He can't face the situation because he does love her, but he honestly feels he has to protect his new family."

Airlie generally lets the script define his character, so

it wasn't until the second season that he decided what type of law Brian practices. "I decided he's a corporate lawyer after Lily calls because Richard was arrested," Airlie notes. "He tells her, 'I'm not a criminal lawyer,' so now I see him working for a multi-national company."

Brian's behavior began to mellow in season two, as Airlie returned for several more appearances. "Andrew is a really fine actor," comments Ira Behr. "And his relationship with Lily got more complicated with time, which was great. If we had ten more minutes of screen-time per week, Brian could have developed into a *fantastic* character."

Considering Lily's fate, Airlie suspects that Brian won't have that opportunity. Still, as one of Airlie's friends on the show told him, "In science fiction, there's no such thing as dead." So who's to say?

April Skouris: Younger sister of Diana Skouris. Tattoo artist and free spirit. — season two production notes

> "Baby girl, you are my new lucky charm."

"April's relationship with Diana is very complicated," observes Natasha Gregson Wagner, the actress who portrays the free spirit. "I think she adores and worships Diana but has always suffered from this feeling of being less than her. I really appreciate April's struggle to be her own person, despite the fact that she makes the wrong choices a lot of the time."

Wagner wasn't familiar with the show when she went in to read for April. "Sometimes you can kind of read the response in the room," she explains. "But after this audition, everyone was really quiet. I left, thinking, 'Well, that was nothing.' But a few hours later they offered me the part, so I guess I must have illuminated something about April that they connected to!"

"We wanted to find the wild child — pretty much the opposite of what we'd created in Diana," says Ira Behr. "In my dad's day, they called them 'free spirits', which could mean players, or even sluts. Natasha had this quality to her, a sexuality, to be sure, but also a vulnerable side. We didn't want someone who seemed to be having *too* good a time playing the field. Natasha was a slam dunk."

Once Wagner had the role, she did a surprisingly in-depth psychoanalysis of her alter ego. "I knew she was an artist, one of those people who have a natural instinct for drawing," she says. "I think she talked herself into becoming a tattoo artist. The medium made sense to her. She was probably a cutter (a self-mutilator) when she was younger, and there's something about tattooing on the flesh that makes her feel alive, the way cutting did. It's not about putting her art on people. It's a way for her to connect flesh to flesh with people."

Wagner reveals that April's brief interaction with Maia had a profound effect on her. "She feels loved by Maia, and honestly seen and accepted by her," she explains. "That's *huge*! She hasn't felt that from a lot of people. It's given her some courage and hope for the future, despite the way things turned out during the visit."

Agent Garrity: NTAC agent in the Northwest office. No first name established. Partnered with Agent Park... until Park shot Director Jarvis.

> **"If there's a space for my signature, it should be MY SIGNATURE!"**

While some viewers may not know who Agent Garrity is, and others may think that his whole reason for existence is to deliver lines of exposition at the NTAC office, you won't find a stauncher advocate for Agent Garrity than Ira Behr — except, perhaps, for actor Kavan Smith.

"I always get a little nervous when you have too many heroes in the pot," explains Behr. "I have a kind of jaundiced view of them. Not everyone's a hero. You need to balance the mix with everyday people. And to me, that's Garrity. He's the anti-Tom Baldwin, the everyman going 'What the f...? There are 4400s with *abilities*? I feel a little overmatched.' It doesn't mean he isn't a good agent — in our minds, he's a very good agent. But he's got a much healthier view of things, given his position."

Smith admits that his character does serve to expedite information on the show. "He helps bounce things off the lead character," Smith says. "Over time, he's become an interesting voice in the room. He's written with a kind of negative spin, so that he comes off like a pessimist, which can be funny. But he's also developed this interesting ability to keep things real. Everything is so heavy when it comes to Tom and Diana, and in the midst of all the usual drama and tragedy and science fiction ideas, it's good to have a character who's not quite as involved."

Smith, the veteran of *Stargate Atlantis*, *Stargate SG-1*, *Battlestar Galactica*, *Twilight Zone* and myriad other series, can also exclusively reveal Garrity's first name — or at least the name that the people on *The 4400* set have given him. "It's Grover," he laughs, "although I doubt very much if that's what the writers will come up with when they finally bestow a *real* name on him." O

Production Design

For producers trying to get new projects off the ground, keeping the budget within a reasonable range always involves compromise. It's a simple fact of show *business*. In the case of *The 4400*, the producers accepted an offer that allowed them to get their 'Pilot' on film. And the trade-off? Accept the basic structure of another show's physical sets, rather than create their own from scratch.

"In trying to figure out how to get the most for our money, I took Maira and Scott to Vancouver and showed them the sets for *Jake 2.0* when that show was shutting down," Perry Simon says. "They said, 'Yes, we can work with this,' and they kind of designed *The 4400* to take advantage of it. It really worked out well."

However, producer Maira Suro has a slightly different memory of the situation. "The facility was terrible. There was nothing nice about it," she says. "But it was standing, so using it offered a very efficient way to be able to produce the show for a price. Luckily, we had a wonderful production designer, Steve Geaghan, who was able to redress everything."

Geaghan, who previously had worked with Scott Peters on *The Outer Limits*, was happy to take up the challenge. "The facility wasn't a soundstage, it was a warehouse," Geaghan says. "But it was a very large space, about 2200 square feet. Unfortunately, I couldn't decipher what the previous sets had been, because the only thing recognizable was a short hallway, and a huge rotunda made of metal and lots of concrete."

Below: The drab surroundings in quarantine helped viewers focus their attention on the characters.

Which was exactly what the Homeland Security set called for. "At first, the rotunda looked great, like eye candy," Suro concedes. "It was the kind of place you imagine a hush-hush governmental agency like Homeland Security would be working out of, so it made sense for the look of NTAC. But shooting in it really was a nightmare. The walls weren't movable, so sometimes it was hard to move the camera around, and the ceiling was so high that the crew always felt as if we were shooting in a vacuum."

"The first thing we did was widen that short hallway and lengthen it another 150 feet," Geaghan says. "And we punched through the walls of the rotunda to build offices. That way we could rotate around the meeting table in Ryland's office and see activity outside. Then we covered the rotunda's walls with a lot more cement and added a huge lit dome over the top. The final set had a visual sense of solidity and well-being that said 'this organization is protected and is protecting us'. And yet it was open enough that the camera could see through it and show a lot of it at once. It was subliminal, but that's the type of thing that Yves Simoneau and I discussed at length."

Lighting was a major concern, Geaghan says, because the show would be shot in high definition. "High-def resolution is so good that you can tell if a painted wall is made of plywood from thirty feet away, or you can see a thumbprint smear in perfect focus six inches from the lens. To deal

with that, cinematographer Tom Burstyn and I installed a lot of permanent recessed lighting throughout the Homeland Security set, along with table lighting that was specific to individual desks and room areas. And we used glass-topped desks and tables so we could put canted florescent lights beneath them to shine upwards into actor's faces.

Above: Diana's organized existence, evidenced by the systematic neatness of her apartment, is challenged by the colorful imagination of a child.

"The other main set for the 'Pilot' was the containment area. We built that in the underside of a local hockey stadium," Geaghan reveals. "Then we painted the whole place very monochromatic. And costume designer Susan de Laval dressed the 4400 in matching monochromatic suits, which lent the whole area a feeling of detachment and control over the people. The suits were just a shade darker than the walls — or maybe it was the other way around."

To portray Highland Beach, the area where the 4400 are returned, "Yves Simoneau chose a very beautiful regional park by Bunsen Lake," the production designer continues. "That took a tremendous amount of work, because it's a fairly public environment, and the beach was covered with dozens of huge concrete picnic tables — which we had to remove."

The other major sets included Linda Baldwin's house and Diana's apartment. "We built Diana's rooms in the warehouse," Geaghan says. "We made it warm and solid, as if she had chosen it carefully. And we decorated it to be tasteful and organized, which is exactly what you want to say about Diana.

"Tom's life, on the other hand, is a mess," Geaghan notes. "To emphasize that, we rented an actual house for the set where his ex-wife lives, and completely repainted it in solid, strong colors to show what Tom had left behind. We redid the kitchen and even landscaped the backyard where Kyle sits under the sprinklers, just to show how much Tom had lost."

Orson Bailey's cabin in the woods, Geaghan reveals, "is an existing cabin only about a hundred feet from the spot where Maia and her parents were having their picnic in the car, and that's about a twenty-minute drive around the lake from where the big returnee scene was. That cabin is in pretty nice shape, so we had to make it look derelict. We added some overgrown bushes and trees; then we broke the gutters and pulled the siding off from a portion of the porch."

For the scenes in which Tom visits his son Kyle in the hospital, the production shot in a working medical facility. "It's called the Rivervale Mental Hospital," Chad Faust relates. "It's a functioning hospital, but a lot of the buildings and wings aren't used anymore, so they're almost exclusively used for filming. In fact, *The X-Files* shot a lot of their shows there. One day I was walking around in my hospital gown with this deathly make-up on. My face and arms were all white and blue, with no pigmentation, because Kyle hadn't had any sun or moved his body in a long time. And I had a head bandage on. Well, there's no division between the open buildings and the rest of the place, so I wandered over into the mental hospital area looking at the patients out on the greens, when I suddenly realized that I could easily be picked up by one of the nurses and taken inside," Faust says wryly, "because I looked just like one of the patients."

"When we shot Carl Morrissey's park, we used an existing playground," Steve Geaghan points out. "But it was small, so we supplemented the jungle gym with wood and metal to make it look more substantial. And we built the memorial with the bust of Lincoln on it from scratch, on an old basketball court. In fact, Suki Parker, our art director, sculpted the bust."

Because the memorial would be seen in various states of disrepair, the art department constructed it in modules, which could be brought in or taken out as the shots demanded. "We built it with pre-stressed panels and tough-backed semi-tacky adhesive paper," the production designer explains. "That way it only took us fifteen minutes to change over from one stage to the next. We had a team of painters standing by, so Yves would shoot a portion and then we'd jump in to get the next shot ready. After a few minutes Yves would step in and they'd shoot again. This is stuff that the audience never knows," Geaghan says, "but it has to be extensively preplanned by the director, the assistant directors and the art department."

With eight days to shoot an episode, scheduling often dictates everything, including location. For instance, on the day the crew shot Carl Morrissey working

NTAC INFORMATION ARCHIVE

"When we have two or three days between scenes on a specific set, we often take those sets down completely and build other sets up in the same area," Ian Thomas says. Why, one wonders, does the crew go to all that trouble, knowing they'll eventually need to rebuild the first set? Simple question, simple answer. "We've run out of space," Thomas explains.

in the supermarket fish department, they also scheduled the scene of Dennis Ryland talking about the case with Tom Baldwin in a restaurant. Normally the scene between Ryland and Tom would have taken place in Ryland's office at NTAC, but there was no time to move back to that set. "The café was in the same block as the grocery," Geaghan says. "It was what we refer to as a 'bastard scene', one that just doesn't fit in with anything else, so we go back to the writers and beg them to change it. Usually there's a lot of hemming and hawing." In this case, the writers were able to justify the café setting because they'd already established that Tom and Ryland are friends away from the office, making a meet over coffee seem plausible.

As for the fish department, "We negotiated use of the whole grocery store for a night, and stripped out a corner," Geaghan explains. "Then we spent the night dressing that corner with our own fish, ice machine and counters. We shot the scene very early in the morning, then moved down the street to the café. The clean-up crew was still working when the store opened and real customers started shopping."

As the second season geared up, Suro says, "We were fortunate, because Kathy Gilroy-Sereda joined our team as a producer, and she's the person who got us into Lion's Gate Studios. She's been a phenomenal partner in Vancouver. It's a much more pleasant place to be, and so much more effective for the show, because we have two huge sound stages. Now the construction crew can be building on one stage while we're shooting on the other. In our first season, there was only one, so every time they called,

Above: Coordination between the production designer, the art director and the property department results in an NTAC office that looks messy but efficient — just like a real office.

Above: Thanks to a little production design ingenuity, viewers would never suspect that Shawn's apartment and Collier's office share the same walls and floor space.

'Action!' all the other work had to stop. It wasn't efficient at all."

"I'm the hands-on gal," Kathy Gilroy-Sereda says. "I was around while we built all the season two sets from scratch. That includes NTAC, the new Baldwin house, Diana's apartment, Collier's office, Shawn's apartment and the theory room. Actually," she reveals, "Collier's office and Shawn's apartment are the same set. We pull out a couple of walls and roll in a couple of flats to transform it. The wall behind Collier's desk is where Shawn's bed sits, and Jordan's office is a little smaller because we put up a flat to hide Shawn's kitchen appliances."

"We basically started with a blank sheet of paper when we designed those sets," second season production designer Ian Thomas says. "We used some photos of the apartments and loosely stayed with the look, but there had been a structural pillar in the middle of Diana's apartment on the old set, and we didn't reproduce that."

"If you look closely, you'll see a post in almost every corner of our sets, or a post half way down a hallway," notes Thomas. "That's because the sets are designed in a 'post and beam' fashion, and the posts can stay when we move 'wild' [removeable] walls. If a set has four walls, at least two of the walls will 'wild out'. We just change the flats between the posts.

"We really redesigned NTAC," the production designer adds. "There were a lot of reasons for that. The gray concrete had given the place a very cold look, so I decided to warm it up by using less concrete and some deep, moody colors, like dark blue

and burgundy. And each office has at least one wall of stained wood. It's still very masculine, but it has more of a corporate look and less of the military feeling it had.

"Instead of the high ceilings, I brought them down quite low. Now when we're shooting in NTAC, you always see the ceiling, which makes it feel subterranean, as if we're underground somewhere," Thomas explains. "We framed the headers in the new ceiling like a web or a maze. In the spaces between the headers we installed one hundred pot lights. So now when the cinematographer goes to the set it's already ninety percent lit.

"It's a really nice set," Thomas says, "with a lot of glass and a lot of wire glass."

The biggest change in the second season sets involves Jordan Collier's newest enterprise, the 4400 Center. "We use an auditorium on the campus of the University of British Columbia," Gilroy-Sereda says. "It's called the Chan Center, and is one of the most acoustically perfect music halls in all of Vancouver."

"Now that's a set that has a lot of concrete in it," Ian Thomas interjects. "The Chan Center is very modern, and very clean. Basically we use the lobby and a long curved hallway. There's a piece of art on the wall of the lobby that we aren't allowed to move, so we cover it with a photograph of the lake and beach where the returnees landed," Thomas explains. "The photograph is on a piece of twenty-foot by twenty-foot canvas. Our DP [director of photography], Tony Westerman, lights it from above so it looks like a big painting.

Above: During the second season, production designer Ian Thomas made the NTAC offices less "military" and more "corporate".

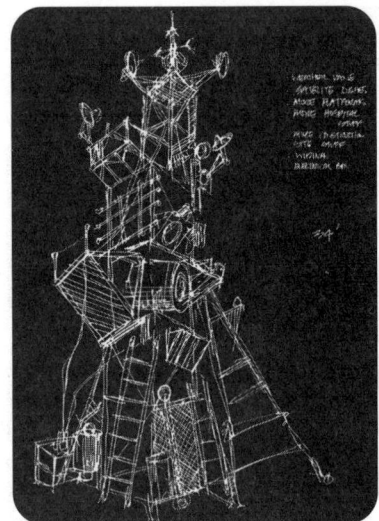

Above: An early production sketch of Tess Doerner's tower was physically realized in 'Wake-Up Call'.

"We cover up a lot of the building's architecture each time we shoot there, so we carry in our own set pieces, like a number of portable concrete walls and a lot of signs."

So far, the production hasn't made use of the Chan Center's main auditorium, but they did find use for the facility's second room, the tri-level Telus Studio Theatre, affectionately referred to locally as the "black box".

"When we were location scouting, we saw the black box theatre and I immediately said, 'Oh my God, I've got to use this,'" Ira Behr recalls enthusiastically. "It's a weird little room with seating towers that can be changed around. So when we shot 'Life Interrupted', that became the future room."

In addition, *The 4400* often shoots exterior scenes in a rose garden near the Chan Center. "The campus is in operation, so when we're filming shows near the end of our season, some scenes can be a little difficult to schedule," Kathy Gilroy-Sereda says. "Every department within the university holds its graduations in the Chan Center. If you look, you'll notice that we don't have a lot of 4400 Center scenes in the episodes we shoot in June."

"The first episode that I worked on, 'Wake-Up Call', was quite challenging," Ian Thomas says, "because we had to build a radio tower at an insane asylum. The way the shot was designed, the tower would be filmed in three stages, so we constructed it in three pieces. But, of course, by the time we got the schedule of actors' availability, we had to shoot stage three first, stage two second and stage one last! Because there was to be a burn sequence, we had to build most of it out of metal. That way, appropriate parts would burn, but the rest of it would be okay for the next — earlier — shot.

"The structure was just a bunch of junk really, old cots and beds and a washing machine drum. And I had the set decorators go to wrecking yards that specialize in electronics and things like that," Thomas says. "Each section was about eight feet high, so the tower stood twenty-four feet all together. We constructed the three pieces at Lion's Gate Studios and moved them to the asylum on three trucks. It took us about ten days to build, and we had a welding crew on set while we shot it.

"And one of the satellite dishes had to turn," Thomas points out, "so we hooked it up to a little electric motor."

"The radio tower served almost as a character itself," Jeffrey Combs recalls. "Somehow it gave my character a paddle shock to the brain instead of the heart, and Kevin was standing there saying, 'I feel... better.'" ○

Music

"The 4400 is about real people caught in surreal circumstances," explains George S. Clinton, composer of the musical score for the 'Pilot'. "Yves Simoneau and I wanted the music to address the human element more than the science fiction element because that's what the 'Pilot' emphasized. For instance, when viewers meet the little girl, Maia, there's something sad about her situation, so I wrote a theme for her in a minor key, using a celesta, which has almost a toy piano sound, along with female voices that sound childlike. It reflects the fact that Maia no longer fits in, and the haunting quality conveys her very human longing.

"The abduction scenes, conversely, tell the science fiction element. People see a bright light and they're suddenly gone," Clinton says. "Because the audience didn't know what was happening, the music had to sell the drama, the feeling that this was truly supernatural and horrible. I didn't want that music to sound wondrous — I wanted it to sound dangerous."

Above: The musical theme written for Maia in the 'Pilot' is one of the few themes to survive into later seasons.

Using his library of what he refers to as "very convincing orchestral and choral samples, along with artificial sounds," Clinton used his keyboard and computer to score the opening abductions with "a palette of surreal sounds." And then he wrote several additional themes.

As with Maia, Clinton wanted different themes and instrumentation to follow various other characters through the 'Pilot'. "For Shawn, I used strange guitar sounds and modified them into indistinguishable growls," Clinton says. "You can't tell what it is, but it's very intense. And sometimes I added drums to that, especially during the fight at the school."

For Lily and Richard's theme, Clinton wrote a complete musical piece — and then deconstructed it. "It's a piano solo played with an orchestra and a lot of oboe," he comments. "The first time you hear it is when Richard's looking at that strip of pictures. But the music is incomplete, because it's not Lily in the picture, it's her grandmother. So after every two or three notes, I took out a couple of notes. As we get to know the two characters, I started putting notes back in, because some of the notes belong to him and some belong to her. It isn't until they finally come together in that park that all the notes are there."

"I didn't write a theme for the detectives, Tom and Diana," Clinton says. "Instead, I played the emotion of each situation they were in. For instance, when they're sneaking up on Orson Bailey's house, I created a growing suspense. But I did write a Homeland Security theme, using a snare drum and a sharp synthesized beat with a lot of electronic delay in it. It's very military," he explains.

"Every time a supernatural event occurred in the 'Pilot', I used one theme — the same theme for all of them. It's an ambient voice and string sound. So even though the scenes are very different, when Shawn almost sucks the life out of that boy, the music is similar to when Maia is sitting there knowing that her foster parents are going to send her back."

Clinton also created atmospheric cues to emphasize important moments in the story. "There's a cue when the 4400 are released from quarantine that's almost a waltz," he points out, "but it has an otherworldly quality to it, a sense of joy but also a sense of not knowing what's going to happen to these people. It's the French horns in that cue that sell the feeling."

And he wrote several longer pieces of music, including one that Clinton named 'Backyard'. "At the beginning of the 'Pilot', Dennis Ryland says, 'My God, they're coming down right in our own backyard,'" the composer relates. "That whole scene — the light coming in, people gathering at the lake, and the 4400 appearing on the beach — is one piece of music. It's a combination of orchestra and chorus, with a hollow kind of voice, but an alien voice that seems to fall in pitch, almost like a distant cry, along with a strange metallic sound that came from bowing the edge of a cymbal with a bass bow."

To end 'Backyard', the composer created the intriguing musical move that viewers hear each week as the opening credits end. "That's the choral voices going up, doing a glissando," Clinton explains. "When people ask a question, their voices tend to go up at the end. I thought it would be interesting to leave, at that point, a question mark in the ears of the audience."

"Yves and I have done a number of pilots together," Clinton says, "but going on with an entire series keeps you locked into the job, and I was contracted to do several feature films. It was great that I was allowed to establish the original voice of the music, and then to hear some of my themes carried on in later episodes."

While the 'Pilot' was being shot, *The 4400*'s producers began their search for a theme song that would give the series an identity. "We had liked 'Worry About You', by the band Ivy," Maira Suro comments, "and we pursued using it, but it already had been used as a theme for something else, so we played it under a montage in the 'Pilot' instead. But that recording sort of influenced the feel that we wanted. We put a call out to a whole bunch of different people, and we got back about twenty choices of songs," Suro says. "In the end we chose 'A Place In Time' by Stephen Phillips and Tim P.".

NTAC INFORMATION ARCHIVE

"Initially, I treated the episode 'Lockdown' as if it were a Hollywood movie," composer John Van Tongeren says. "The first time around, I created an action-oriented film score, with a lot of brass and big sounds. But after I sent it to the producers, Ira made me pull it back a little. I think he worried that I was overdriving a bit," the composer recalls with a chuckle, "because he accused me of 'going Bruckheimer' on him."

"The producers gave us a one-sentence synopsis of *The 4400* and asked, 'Can you give us sixty seconds of music with lyrics?'" says Phillips, who with his writing partner Tim P., is co-founder of music firm BossHouse Music. "Based on that short synopsis, the line 'a place in time' seemed like a proper metaphor for the show. We wrote it in one day."

"Steve played guitar and I played drums and bass, and we both played some keyboards on it," Tim P. says. "We wrote the song on a Thursday, including the lyrics, and on Friday morning we asked our friend Amanda Abizaid to come up and sing it. We thought that her voice would fit the bill, and it did."

Singer, composer and musician Amanda Abizaid is a consummate artist whose work can be heard on her own DVDs as well as on her website, www.amandaabizaid.com. Most of the time she enjoys a trip to the studio, but on this particular day she was feeling under the weather. "I decided to go in anyway," she says, "but when I got there, I just sat down. Tim and Stephen played a rough track of the music a couple of times to give me the feel of the song. Usually I stand up when I record, but because I wasn't feeling well, I thought, 'I'll just keep sitting while I sing this.' I wasn't in the best mood, and I only used my speaking voice range, not pushing it, just real light and airy, and real laid back," Abizaid adds. "I was only there for forty-five minutes and then I went home.

"As I was leaving, they were saying, 'Aw, it's not gonna happen, but thanks for doing this, at least we got a cool song,'" the singer remembers, laughing. "But as it turned out, it was a great song that ended up going really far. Of course, at sixty seconds, it's only half a song…"

Above: Scenes without dialogue offer the composers much-appreciated opportunities to create longer pieces of music.

Above: The music that accompanies several of Richard and Lily's scenes contains a combination of notes the composer originally assigned to each of them individually.

As George Clinton moved on to other projects, the producers turned their attention to finding composers for the rest of their miniseries. Standard procedure on most television series is for two composers to share the musical duties, alternating on every other episode in order to have maximum time for writing and recording. The producers were very happy to learn that two of their top choices were available: Claude Foisy (*White Noise, Ghost Stories, The Boxer, 2001: A Space Travesty*) and John Van Tongeren (*The Outer Limits, Poltergeist: The Legacy, Miss Congeniality 2: Armed and Fabulous*).

"When I started on 'The New and Improved Carl Morrisey', the producers pretty much left me to my own devices, except for asking me to quote Maia's theme and Richard and Lily's theme," Claude Foisy says. "I got my inspiration from watching the episode and translating it into musical terms. I'm a pianist, so I have a fondness for keyboards, and I'm more fond of strings than brass. But I also like to combine those traditional sounds with more science fiction type sounds, which is perfect for *The 4400.*"

John Van Tongeren feels similarly. "I think it's better to lean more toward the otherworldly musical feeling on the show," he says. "The producers were happy with the tone that George had set in the 'Pilot', so I used that as a jumping-off point on my first episode, 'Becoming'. Of course, the Maia theme is pretty identifiable, and we all liked it. Good one, George!"

Like Clinton, Van Tongeren found himself playing to the emotional thrust of scenes as a whole, because "scenes often are more situational than character-driven," he says. "I do have little motifs for some of the characters, like Isabelle, but they're small little fragments, not full-on *Doctor Zhivago* melodies. Since Isabelle's emotions can be all over the place, her motif is pretty malleable."

While Foisy and Van Tongeren have similar tasks, they each find that they still can maintain their individual, identifiable styles. "I'm sure that if someone listens really carefully, he or she might pick up on certain threads of what I like to do," Foisy says. "For instance, I use a theme for the returnees that is kind of minimalist and repetitive. It's mostly acoustic sounding, and almost lyrical."

A good example of Foisy's minimalist sound is in the season two opener, 'Wake-Up Call'. "I used minimalism because it seemed that the people building the tower were kind of going in circles. So I gave the score a repetitive quality, like a Philip Glass piece, with a lot of sound design things mixed with piano and strings."

The alternating episode pattern landed John Van Tongeren on the unique episode 'Life Interrupted'. "I tried to create an alternate reality musical environment for Tom to work in," Van Tongeren says. "I used a lot of bowed percussion instruments. I was lucky enough to find samples of bowed vibraphone, which were made by running a bass bow up the flat edge of the vibes bars. And bowed antique cymbals called crotales, and bowed gongs. These instruments normally are struck with a mallet, but the bowing didn't give any 'attack' to the notes, so everything had a *legato*, smooth tone.

"The future room had the most synthetic sound," Van Tongeren continues. "For those scenes, I created a really thick texture with synthesizers as opposed to the bowed acoustic sounds, to keep it separate. There's a lot of modulating going on, things moving around inside the sound, so the room was in an ever revolving musical landscape. And I put a string line on top that kept escalating to keep the tension going. It's what I call a 'hybrid score'," Van Tongeren says. "It just sounds very otherworldly."

The personality of the show's recurring characters also inspired unique sounds. "I've scored a couple of fun scenes with Marco," Claude Foisy says with a smile. "His music usually ends up being more 'techno' oriented than the rest, because Marco operates on a different, more nerdy level than the other characters. I use what could be construed as computer noises, so it's certainly less acoustic sounding."

The longest piece of music regularly played on the series is titled 'Salvation', written by John Van Tongeren. Although it now plays at the start of every episode, the composition first was heard in 'As Fate Would Have It', when the producers added a new feature to the show. Known in the business as a "saga sell", it's a montage that explains the premise of the series to the television audience, particularly those viewers who may be tuning in for the first time. "I'm really proud of 'Salvation'," Van Tongeren says. "It seems to have captured the spirit of the show, and it plays really well on television — clean and balanced. I hope that when it comes on, anyone who hears it will think, 'Ahh, *The 4400*.'" ○

THE 4400 SONG LIST

Music supervisor Elliot Lurie is assigned the task of choosing and legally acquiring the use of songs that will enhance an episode's soundtrack. "There are two categories of songs in the series," Lurie explains, "those that act like a score over a scene or a montage, and those that we call 'source', which are meant to be emanating from a musical device, like a radio. The second type usually relates to the characters in the scene and are age appropriate.

"When a new script comes in, the writers may indicate that a scene should be covered by a song, or they may even suggest a title, although that doesn't happen very often," Lurie notes. "Otherwise, I will suggest possible scenes for songs. Based on the script, I begin looking for appropriate, available material."

The following songs have been compiled by Lurie, and used during the first two seasons of *The 4400*:

Amanda Abizaid 'A Place In Time': Theme song

PILOT
Billie Holiday 'Cheek to Cheek': Maia and her parents in the car
Ivy 'Worry About You': Montages

THE NEW AND IMPROVED CARL MORRISSEY
Insolence 'Poison Well': Carl Morrissey's cleanup/fight in the park
Nat King Cole 'Mona Lisa': Richard and Lily dancing together
Hoobastank 'The Reason': Shawn and Nikki in the garage
Los Lonely Boys 'Heaven': In the market where Carl works

BECOMING
Seals & Croft 'Summer Breeze ('04 Remix)': In the bar

TRIAL BY FIRE
Engineers 'How Do You Say Goodbye?': Nikki breaking up with Danny
Maroon 5 'She Will Be Loved': Shawn and Nikki at the return site

WHITE LIGHT
Staind 'It's Been a While': Danny gives Nikki the earrings/Diana goes to pick up Maia from daycare
Incubus 'Talk Shows On Mute': Shawn and Nikki in the car

WAKE-UP CALL
Ryan Cabrara 'True': Diana and Maia's celebration dinner
Bedroom Walls 'Do the Buildings and Cops Make You Smile?': End montage

VOICES CARRY
Alison Krauss & Union Station 'Gravity': Richard and Lily check in to the hotel

WEIGHT OF THE WORLD
DJ Z-Trip feat. Chester Bennington 'Walking Dead': Maia, Diana and April at the tattoo parlor
Bloc Party 'Banquet': Kyle at the party
Elkland 'Everybody's Leaving'

SUFFER THE CHILDREN
(Classical music only)

AS FATE WOULD HAVE IT
Paul Trudeau 'You Are': Maia, Diana and April making dinner
The Kills 'I Hate the Way You Love': Kyle at the concert
Kasabian 'Running Battle': End montage

LIFE INTERRUPTED
Chet Baker 'Time After Time': Tom and Alana's wedding reception
Lifehouse 'You & Me': Tom chases after Alana

CARRIER
Randy Travis 'Three Wooden Crosses': Jean Baker and the trucker driving toward Seattle

REBIRTH
Charles Brown 'Route 66': Richard and his army buddies at the bar

HIDDEN
Queens of the Stone Age 'Little Sister': Shawn and Danny washing the car

LOCKDOWN
Jet 'Look What You've Done': Kyle and Molly get better acquainted

MOMMY'S BOSSES
Jacqueline McKenzie 'Shy Baby': Diana and Marco kiss
Switchfoot 'This Is Your Life': End montage

Visual Effects

"It's my least favorite moment in *4400* history," Kaj-Erik Eriksen says. "For the scenes in the 'Pilot' where Brooke and I were standing on the street watching the comet come in, it was supposed to be nighttime, but it actually was broad daylight. We were shooting 'day for night', which means that the visual effects people would color-correct the film later on to make it look like night. We had to stare right into the bloody sun — which is why I look all scrunch-faced. My eyes were just burning and watering," Eriksen grimaces. "Shooting that scene was brutal."

During the early episodes, the budget called all the shots, or at least the scheduling, which ruled out costly night shooting. "In the beginning, when everything was on the line, we had to cut corners," Ira Behr admits, "and it showed in the production values. When the crew shot those scenes, they made sure to shoot a cardboard sign that explained to the people watching dailies, 'This is being shot during the day for night, but it'll look great once we twist the dials.' But it never looked great, and I felt a little embarrassed," Behr sighs. "Getting the miniseries off the granite was pretty rocky."

The first season demanded a substantial amount of work from the visual effects team, led at the time by FX supervisor Jim Finn (*Life As We Know it*, *Gene Roddenberry's Andromeda*). It included color-correcting those pseudo night scenes in the 'Pilot' and 'The New and Improved Carl Morrissey'. And that included rotoscoping (tracing around, pixel by pixel) everything that was white, or that glowed with light, such as windows and auto headlight beams, so that they wouldn't appear blue.

Finn also was responsible for entire sequences that would make or break the series' chance for success — such as the ball of light that brings the returnees home. "We wanted the ball of light to resemble organic material, pumping and moving like a big heart," director Yves Simoneau says. "The idea was that it wasn't a space ship, or anything like that. It was like a living but not completely defined liquid sphere inside another

Below: From just two lines in the script, "A glowing object" and "The ball of light", the visual effects team created an intriguing, undulating vision.

Above: Don't bother knocking. Richard and Lily's cabin never existed as a physical set — although the wind-chimes were real.

liquid sphere, with an organic and living skin that appeared metallic. The liquid had to be floating, with an outside that kept moving all the time like a soap bubble, and was transparent while emanating light. It was a difficult order for the visual effects guys," Simoneau says admiringly.

"Jim and his team came up with an animated structure with layers that reacted to each other," explains Roberto Biagi (*Gene Roddenberry's Andromeda, Poltergeist: The Legacy*), the visual effects supervisor who took over the reins after the miniseries. "There's a great deal of 3-D liquid dynamics involved, with computer graphics conveying a liquid that can bend and warp within itself. Then they added an element called sub-surface scattering, which adds light inside an object. It's kind of like when you hold a flashlight behind your hand so you can see through the skin. They dealt with layers and layers of that. And they put some little lightning strikes within it."

Less obvious visual effects work appears in every episode, quite often unbeknownst to viewers. For instance, near the end of 'White Light', viewers see a wind-chime hanging on the porch of a cabin where Lily and Richard are staying. But that seemingly ordinary insert shot is anything but. "I sent a camera crew out to film a bushy hilltop," production designer Steve Geaghan says. "Then I found a photograph of a cabin in a magazine and the visual effects guys inserted the photo into the location footage. Then we shot a wind-chime in front of a greenscreen, and Jim Finn inserted the wind-chime so it looks like it's hanging on the porch. The entire shot is artificially created," Geaghan says.

"When we started season two, we wanted to improve on the effects by making them more subtle, yet with more detail in them," says Biagi. "For instance, we do an effect called a 'life suck' — it's when Shawn almost sucks the life out of somebody. In season one, that effect was very pronounced. They did it entirely in 2-D, making the skin go totally white, with gauntly cut cheeks and deep black eyes. But when we did it in 'Voices Carry', we started with orthographic (from all angles) photos of the actor's head and shoulders, and brought it into the 3-D world using a software program called Maya. We mapped a 3-D rendition of his face onto that, which gave us a digital stand-in of his whole head, and we put a subtle glow beneath the skin, creating textures around the eyes. In addition, we used that sub-surface scattering technique so we could see what was happening beneath the skin. We created 3-D models of veins so we could grow and shrink them to make the impression that blood pressure was being blocked in the arteries, affecting the veins. That stuff is on screen for only a few seconds," Biagi concludes, "but the detail really sells the effect and makes it realistic.

"When Lily and Richard are hiding in the woods in 'Wake-Up Call'," Biagi continues, "we had to make berries ripen on a flowering plant. To research the effect, we purchased a very young Oregon grape plant about a month before we would have to do the shot. During the month, we studied it as it grew and flowered. We shot reference plates, and also shot a large silver ball under the same lighting to get the reflections, which gave us the lighting information we'd need. And we used the same camera angle and lens information as the principal photography, so we could match that film footage. Then we took all that information into the 3-D department and rebuilt some of the branches that were around the plant to match the lighting. Finally, we went through the stages of building our plant from the reference plates, creating buds and flowers, texturing and animating them. By the way," Biagi adds, "about a month after we'd finished, our real plant actually developed grapes!

"There's another shot in 'Wake-Up Call', when Lily is in a store. Josiah the fundamentalist comes in, so Isabelle creates a storm. We decorated an empty store as a gift shop, and shot photographic plates. Then we put up a greenscreen in the store and shot Laura Allen and the baby against that, in high-speed so we could get very subtle movements. At that point we had all the actors leave and we removed our greenscreen. Then the physical special effects team turned on these massive fans and blowers, and just basically blew the place apart," Biagi says with a smile. "We composited those layers of film together to get the basic footage, and later we set up a greenscreen on a soundstage, turned on a high speed camera, and threw all kinds of paper products and debris in front of the greenscreen. We had to rotoscope a lot of the paper in order to make it appear to go behind the actors, but it was worth the trouble. We also blew up a lot of great little props, like ceramic animals," the visual

Above: Baby Isabelle destroys the shop, with a little help from the combined visual effects and physical special effects teams.

effects supervisor remembers fondly. "There was one little ceramic pig that we had tumble across and blow up right in the middle of the frame. It blew up real good. That was cool."

One episode in which viewers can't miss the visual effects was 'Life Interrupted'. There are two major effects sequences: one where Tom sees the future room shatter around him; and another near the end when the alternate world disappears around Tom and Alana. "Ira Behr wanted the future room to appear to shatter as if it was a reflection in a breaking mirror," Biagi says. "First we shot a ton of plates inside the University of British Columbia's black box theatre. Then we shot Joel Gretsch's reflection in a mirror, from a low, low angle with the POV actually beneath his feet. And we also shot Joel in front of a greenscreen. We wanted major movement in the greenscreen shot, so we put Joel on an automated lazy Susan. As he was spinning one way, the lazy Susan was mounted on a moving stand that made it go in circles the other way. And we put the camera on a jib arm attached to a dolly so it could go up and down and side to side. Believe me, there were tracking markers all over the greenscreen," Biagi points out. "And we had orange balls on stands to help us track the shot, because the camera was moving all over the place.

"When we had the footage, my team of artists recreated the future room background more as a matte painting than a 3-D creation," he continues. "We stitched together layers of photography, kind of like tiles, and brought that into a 3-D space. Then we mapped that onto the inside of a sphere, so once we tracked the camera, we could rotate everything to every angle we needed. The idea was for the shot to seem really insane and off-balance. We ended up shattering that background apart in 3-D, and then we added multiple 2-D layers of practical glass shattering. The effect ended up looking really otherworldly," he concludes happily.

In the final shot inside Tom and Alana's alternate universe, their family members disappear, followed by their house and the entire neighborhood. Notes Biagi, "We didn't want to do just an old-fashioned lock-off, where you stop the camera, have the actor step away and then shoot again. So we approached it by having each of the characters dissolve out, which is much more difficult.

"Michael Watkins, the director, wanted part of the sequence to be a moving shot," the visual effects supervisor explains. "So we brought in a motion control unit with a moving camera head. That allowed us to pan, tilt and zoom, and remember the moves. We lined up the actors and did the easy ones first. Diana was standing behind the couch, so the director called 'Freeze,' and she just took off. But the shot where Shawn disappears is different," Biagi explains. "He had a glass in his hand, and he was overlapping Kyle — plus, he's sitting on the couch, squishing the cushion down. So we had to rebuild the cushion once he's gone, and have it warp as if someone's weight just came off it. It was subtle, but it had to be done, or the audience would have been pulled out of the story.

"The toughest one was where Danny and his wife Nikki disappear. That was the motion control shot. Kaj had his arm around Brooke's shoulder, but they disappear separately. It was hard to keep them lined up, so later we had to do a lot of rotoscoping. We had to 'eyeball' lining them back up after each take, and it took about ten times to get it right — and even then we had to recreate Kaj's hand later on. We used somebody else's hand, of course," admits Biagi, "and just painted it over her shoulder."

But the most complicated shot in the episode was when Alana and Tom leave their home and walk away from the alternate reality. "It's a tracking shot with the camera dollying across the frame to find Joel and Karina as they walk toward it, and then everything behind them disappears," comments Biagi. "I'm a big fan of anatomy, not just in people, but in objects," he adds. "I like the way structures are built, like the framework of a car with the engine beneath, or a house with

Below: The visual effects team discovered that getting rid of an entire family can be tougher than expected.

Above: The enemy within Kyle Baldwin.

framework under the bricks. So I really wanted to attack the shot with that in mind — even though we only had two weeks to do the entire disappearance sequence. First we laid half a block of dolly track so we could shoot along a whole row of houses. We did sixteen passes with the camera on that dolly. The first pass was of our actors. For the next one, we removed a parked car, and then we slowly removed objects between passes, like flower pots, or chairs from porches. Because we weren't using greenscreen we knew we'd have to rotoscope like crazy, particularly because we had a car drive down the street in one pass, and people walk by in another.

"Then we put the footage into the computer and started building layers," Biagi continues. "The artists created a simple matte painting of the sky, and one artist shot time-lapse footage of clouds. We built a 3-D framework and put studs inside the houses, and plumbing pipes, and frames and engines of cars, so as they disappeared, they disappeared in layers. There was a large tree on the street, and I got a lot of major grief about that from the artists. The tree had to be rotoscoped right down to the leaves. People wanted to strangle me," laughs Biagi, "but I just told them that they were lucky it hadn't been windy!

"There's so much going on in that sequence that you'd have to watch it twenty times to catch it all," Biagi says. "It actually looks quite simple, but there are layers and layers of images on top of each other, just disappearing. When we were done, there were over eighty layers in all.

"I like to put as much movement in the effects as possible," Biagi relates, "and I got to do that when Kyle sees his split image in the mirror in 'Weight of the World'.

We started with a steadycam shot over Chad's shoulder as he stares at his reflection. That shot had to be tracked into a 3-D space, which was rather expensive. Then we shot Chad in front of a greenscreen. We made him do every movement known to man, including breakdancing, and appearing to have a seizure. Chad was sweating like a banshee, and I'll bet he lost a few pounds by the end of it!"

"We composited that footage over the mirror reflection and created it with in between morphs and layers of anatomy. We scanned lots of anatomical models, like muscles and skeletal structure from really old-fashioned anatomy books, and put them in as flashes every few seconds, until there were about twenty-five layers composing the shot."

In the season's final episode, 'Mommy's Bosses', Kyle finally gets rid of the future being living inside of him, thanks to an assist by his cousin Shawn. "We shot Chad from every angle in front of a greenscreen with a still camera, and built his head and shoulders in 3-D so we could do the life suck effect," Biagi notes. "We painted all the

Below: In Shawn's capable hands, Kyle finally is rid of the entity living inside him.

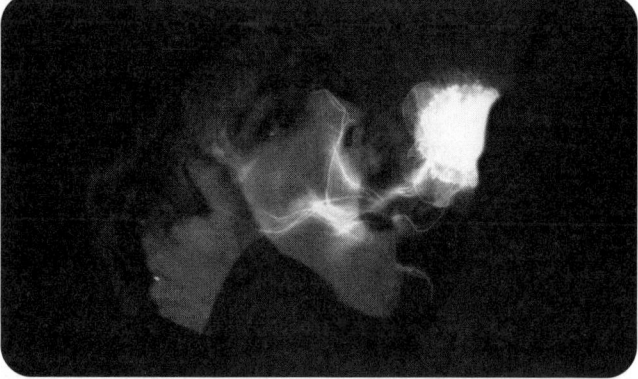

textures of his lips and eyes, and had the veins in his eyes go bloodshot, followed by the veins in his face. Then we had a kind of 'electrical force', for lack of a better term, come out of his mouth. We wanted that to look somewhat like the ball of light from the 'Pilot', but we wanted to take it up a step, to another level. So as that electrical force forms into a small ball of light between Kyle and Shawn, an undulating tentacle-like form comes out of his mouth and spirals around his head. That's the entity that was living inside Kyle. The ball of light is an energy source that pulls the entity into it.

"At one point, there's a flash of a 3-D face among those tentacles," the visual effects supervisor adds. "We had discussions with the producers about what the future people might look like, and how much we could reveal. In the end it's just a quick flash, and it's pretty nondescript. But the concept was great." ○

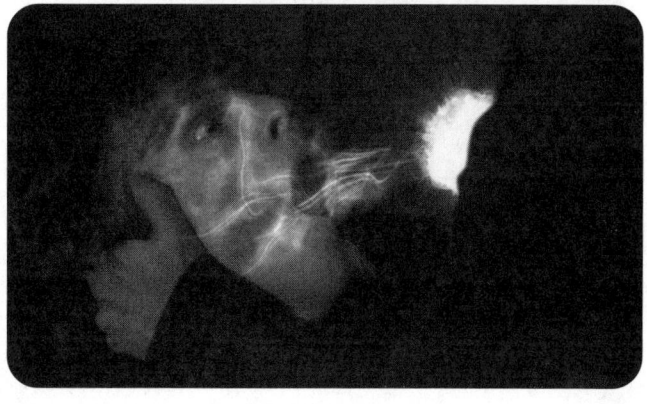

I used to work for someone in the business, who when asked how he was doing, would reply, "Livin' the dream." At the time, he was an out of work actor/comedian, on his fourth pot of coffee for the day, and in the middle of writing a screenplay. He was being funny, but also kind of serious. Those words still ring in my ears. And here's why...

It's funny how when you create a series, you really are like someone in the middle of a dream. Your mind conjures up the characters, the situations, the dialogue, the plot twists, the production design. Writing is like working on a waking dream. You work for months on end, getting everything just right. You get to know your characters really well, but no matter how fleshed out they are, they're still just figments of the imagination.

Then one day you get a greenlight and you get to cast these characters. And overnight they become flesh and blood. You can go out to dinner with them, they have voices, they have distinct laughs, you get a hug from them at the end of a long work day — they've become reality. Okay, yes, technically you're going out to dinner with the actors portraying your characters, but if you allow yourself a momentary indulgence, and you look around at everyone seated — you can easily convince yourself otherwise. Just for fun, and just for a moment, you don't see Joel, you see Tom. That's not Jacqui, that's Diana. And no that's not Patrick pushing Chad down the street in a shopping cart at two in the morning (which really happened), that's Shawn and his cousin Kyle. And you think, "Jesus, am I dreaming? Did I dream them up or am I a part of their dream?"

Okay, so now once they're all cast, then you go to work. You place them in the settings you've dreamed up. And they say the words that create the relationships and twist the plot and manipulate our emotions — words that you gave them. And instantly for that take — they ARE them. And you do this day in and day out for the entire shooting schedule.

And as you start to edit the episodes, the dream really comes to life. You can manipulate the characters — what they do; how they say things. You add visual effects, and sound effects and music. And suddenly the dream is fully realized. That same day, you go and hang out with these folks at some get-together, and you look around the room, and it feels like you really *are* entrenched in the dream. It's as if you've created not just a show but a new reality. It's as if a viewer (me) was allowed into the TV tube to hang out with his favorite TV characters.

And then the shooting schedule begins to wind down, and you look up and suddenly Lily's not there anymore. And neither is Maia. And Kyle is now gone, and so is Jordan Collier. And has anyone seen Richard or Ryland? I said goodbye to Shawn this morning. And then only Tom and Diana are left, and soon enough, they're gone too. All of the characters just disappear. It's as if you are waking up. And you look around like a mamma dog for her puppies, but they're not there — one by one, taken away and sent off to new homes. And there are no more dinners and there's no more hanging out. All you have left is your memory of the dream (in episodic form). You can tell your friends and family all about your dream; hell if you have a DVD player you can do one better and *show* them your dream. But now you're awake. You're back in Los Angeles where you live, not in that make-believe land (Vancouver) where the dream actually took place. Back in the real world — until next season and the process starts all over again. It all goes by in the blink of an eye, while at the same time taking for-freakin-ever. Just like a dream does.

So now when we're shooting *The 4400* and someone asks me how I'm doing, I look at them, I smile, I say, "I'm fine," and we move on. I purposely don't steal my former boss' line in replying. I don't use his line, but sometimes I think it — I really am living the dream.

Scott Peters
Creator/Executive Producer
January 2007